The United States and the Persian Gulf

Reshaping Security Strategy
for the Post-Containment Era

The United States and the Persian Gulf

Reshaping Security Strategy for the Post-Containment Era

edited by Richard D. Sokolsky

NATIONAL DEFENSE UNIVERSITY PRESS
WASHINGTON, D.C.
2003

The opinions, conclusions, and recommendations expressed or implied within are those of the contributors and do not necessarily represent the views of the Department of Defense or any other agency or department of the Federal Government. This publication is cleared for public release; distribution unlimited.

Portions of this work may be quoted or reprinted without further permission, with credit to the Institute for National Strategic Studies. A courtesy copy of any reviews and tearsheets would be appreciated.

Library of Congress Cataloging-in-Publication Data
 The United States and the Persian Gulf : reshaping security strategy for the
  post-containment era / edited by Richard D. Sokolsky.
   p. cm.
Includes bibliographical references.
 ISBN 1–57906–062–5
 1. Middle East—Relations—United States. 2. United
States—Relations—Middle East. 3. War on Terrorism, 2001– 4. United
States—Politics and government—2001– 5. Iraq—Politics and
government—1991– I. Sokolsky, Richard.
  DS63.2.U5U543 2003
  327.73056'09'0511—dc21   2003000089

First Printing, February 2003

NDU Press publications are sold by the U.S. Government Printing Office. For ordering information, call (202) 512–1800 or write to the Superintendent of Documents, U.S. Government Printing Office, Washington, D.C. 20402. For GPO publications on-line access their Web site at: http://www.access.gpo.gov/su_docs/sale.html.

For current publications of the Institute for National Strategic Studies, consult the National Defense University Web site at: http://www.ndu.edu.

Contents

Preface

As this book goes to press in early 2003, U.S.-led military action to eliminate Iraqi weapons of mass destruction and to create postwar conditions that could support democratic political development appears increasingly likely. However that operation unfolds, it will mark an end to the decade-long policy of containment of Iraq and set the stage for a new American approach to security cooperation and political engagement throughout the Persian Gulf. The chapters in this book offer a timely and sustainable roadmap for a new U.S. strategy and military posture in the region.

The presence of U.S. forces in the Persian Gulf, particularly in Saudi Arabia, has been a highly contentious issue in the Arab world since the Persian Gulf War of 1991. While this presence gave the United States and its coalition partners new flexibility in containing Saddam Husayn, managing regional stability, and ensuring access to oil, it also exacerbated anti-American sentiment, particularly among the more devout and disaffected youth in the region. Removal of that presence and of the governments that allowed it became a rallying cry for Osama bin Laden and in the development of the terrorist *jihad* of al Qaeda. However, as contributors to this volume make clear, even in the absence of the new demands of the global war on terrorism, other regional political and strategic developments, as well as the erosion of international support for dual containment, warrant a reshaping of that military presence. Moreover, the continued transformation of U.S. military forces, including the enhancement of expeditionary and long-range power projection capabilities, could allow for a reduced forward presence in the Gulf.

Managing such a transition will require a comprehensive regional strategy and reduction of the Iraqi threat to the region. Washington's scope for action will be greatly influenced by how military action against Iraq unfolds and what conclusions other countries in the region draw from it. But the contributors to this volume make a compelling case that regardless of the nature of regime change in Iraq, there are persuasive political and geostrategic reasons for the United States to make major changes in its military posture and regional security strategy. Equally important, the contributors offer principles for effective promotion of the political and economic reforms that are essential to addressing the root causes of terrorism and many of the region's fundamental problems.

Stephen J. Flanagan
Director, Institute for National Strategic Studies
and Vice President for Research
National Defense University

Acknowledgments

I wish to thank my colleagues in the Institute for National Strategic Studies (INSS) at the National Defense University (NDU), both past and present, for their contributions to this study. INSS convened a series of working group meetings on Persian Gulf security in 2001 to examine the trends shaping the regional security environment and their implications for U.S. security strategy and force posture in the Persian Gulf. I am grateful to the following individuals for their presentations and participation at these sessions: Rachel Bronson, Council on Foreign Relations; Stephen Grummon; Emile Nakleh; James Placke, Cambridge Energy Research Associates; Kenneth Pollack, The Brookings Institution; Paul Pillar; Harold R. Rooks; James Russell; Stephen Ward; Wayne White; and Jeffrey K. Wichman.

I owe a special thanks to F. Gregory Gause of the University of Vermont for his many helpful suggestions on the manuscript and to James A. Schear, director of research at INSS, and Stephen J. Flanagan, director of INSS, for their guidance and sage counsel in shepherding the manuscript to completion.

My thanks go as well to Toshi Yoshihara at the Institute for Foreign Policy Analysis for his contribution to chapter six and to Kathleen Ridolfo and Irene Tragos for their research assistance and help in organizing the Persian Gulf study group sessions.

Thanks are due to the editorial staff of National Defense University Press—General Editor William R. Bode and editors George C. Maerz, Lisa M. Yambrick, and Jeffrey D. Smotherman—who brought this publication to completion under the supervision of Robert A. Silano, director of publications.

This study is the result of a truly collaborative endeavor and would not have been possible without the time, knowledge, and wisdom contributed by a number of academic and U.S. Government experts on the Persian Gulf and greater Middle East. While their contributions were of enormous value, I bear sole responsibility for the final product.

The United States and the Persian Gulf

Reshaping Security Strategy for the Post-Containment Era

Chapter One

Introduction

Richard D. Sokolsky

Significant changes lie ahead for U.S. security strategy in the Persian Gulf after almost a decade of stasis. In the decade between the Gulf War and the terrorist attacks on the World Trade Center and the Pentagon, the strategy of dual containment of Iraq and Iran was a key driver of American military planning and force posture for the region. During these years, the overriding U.S. concern was preserving access to Gulf oil at reasonable prices; both Iran and Iraq possessed only a limited ability to project power and influence beyond their borders; the Persian Gulf states acquiesced to a significant U.S. military presence on their soil despite the domestic costs; and the United States was reasonably successful, at least until the second Palestinian *intifada* in September 2000, in insulating its relationships with key Gulf states from the Israeli-Palestinian conflict.

At the end of the Clinton administration, it seemed safe to assume that the regional security environment would continue to evolve more or less on its present trajectory and that the challenge confronting the United States was how to manage U.S. forward presence for the long haul under increasingly stressful conditions. This premise is no longer valid. The strategy of dual containment, which is just barely alive, will expire in one way or another in all likelihood because the United States decides to end Saddam Husayn's rule. American success in engineering a regime change in Baghdad will require a substantial increase in U.S. forward deployed forces followed by a multinational occupation of Iraq that is likely to include a significant U.S. military component.

At the same time, even if regime change does not occur in Iraq, other factors are likely to put pressure on the United States over the next decade to alter the shape of its military posture toward the region. The campaign against global terrorism will demand a closer look at U.S. policies toward the Persian Gulf that complicate this effort, including the U.S. military presence. Political and social trends in Saudi Arabia will make the royal family even more wary of U.S. forces on their soil. Iran and Iraq are

3

likely to improve their conventional capabilities and, more importantly, to deploy nuclear, biological, and chemical (NBC) weapons and longer-range ballistic missiles to threaten U.S. access and force projection capabilities. The demands of the war on terrorism and American defense strategy more broadly could make sustaining current military commitments in the region increasingly difficult. Finally, the transformation of U.S. military capabilities is likely to create new opportunities to enhance force projection capabilities with fewer forward deployed forces.

With or without regime change in Iraq, the U.S. military posture toward the region will become increasingly brittle unless it adapts in creative ways to these looming changes. On the one hand, if the Gulf security environment stays on its present trajectory—continued deterioration and eventual collapse of dual containment and no American effort to change the geopolitical landscape—the central dilemma facing U.S. policymakers will be reconciling the military requirements of a containment strategy with the political imperatives of reducing the American military profile in the Gulf. On the other hand, the elimination of Iraq as a strategic threat, or the installation of a new but still antagonistic regime, would confront the United States with a number of complex and novel policy issues: the role of Saudi Arabia in U.S. regional security strategy, the degree to which a friendly and pro-American Iraq could become the focus of U.S. regional defense strategy, and the type of military presence the United States should maintain in the region if the removal of the Saddam regime ushers in a period of prolonged instability and disorder inside Iraq and beyond.

The purpose of this study is to evaluate the implications of these political, strategic, security, and military factors for U.S. military presence and force posture, defense and security relationships, and force planning for the region. Specifically, the chapters that follow seek to frame the issues, options, and tradeoffs facing U.S. defense planners by focusing on the following questions:

- To what extent does the emerging security environment—that is, the changing nature of U.S. interests and threats to those interests—require changes in the size and composition of forward deployed forces, peacetime engagement activities, military operations, and force protection?
- Does the United States need to reconfigure its security and military relationships with regional friends and allies to take account of their changing security perceptions and policies?

- Are there trends in the strategic environment that are likely to generate new demands and requirements for the Armed Forces?
- How can the United States reconcile the call in the Quadrennial Defense Review 2001 for greater flexibility in the global allocation of U.S. defense capabilities with the harsh reality that, for the foreseeable future, forward defense of the Persian Gulf will remain dependent on substantial reinforcements from the United States?

The main conclusion of this study is that, with or without regime change in Iraq, the United States will need to make significant adjustments in its military posture toward the region.

Chapter two provides an overview of U.S. interests and objectives in the Gulf. It addresses the strengths and shortcomings of current policies and explains the choices and tradeoffs that the United States is likely to face in deciding on an appropriate force posture for the region in light of competing strategic priorities and resource constraints. Of particular interest are the principles it lays out for a policy of encouraging political and economic reforms to alleviate the root causes of terrorism and domestic instability without simultaneously unleashing pent-up forces for change that could threaten important U.S. interests and prove difficult to control. The chapter's conclusion that the United States will continue to confront endless security dilemmas and headaches until there is a definitive resolution of the Iraqi problem is an important consideration in the ongoing debate over whether the United States should take military action to unseat Saddam Husayn. The discussion also makes a strong case that regime change in Iraq is critical to U.S. efforts to promote long-term political development because only regime change will permit significant reduction of the U.S. military "footprint" in the region.

Chapter three examines the internal and external factors that will shape the threat perceptions, security doctrines, and military policies of key regional actors. It also looks at the prospects for shifting regional alignments and security relationships and internal developments that could affect U.S. presence, capabilities, and force requirements. The discussion makes clear that a business-as-usual approach to managing the U.S. military footprint in the region, and our security relationships more broadly, is no longer adequate to protect American interests. While many Gulf states are wary of the use of U.S. military force to remove Saddam, they are also weary of providing indefinite military support for a strategy of containment. The judgment that most Gulf states prefer a return to the pre-*Desert Storm* situation, in which a balance of power was maintained by a de facto partnership with

Iraq backed by a more distant over-the-horizon U.S. presence, has important implications for U.S. operational planning for defense of the region.

Chapter four assesses the long-term trends in the regional military balance with particular emphasis on prospects for Iraqi and Iranian acquisition of weapons of mass destruction and the ability of the Gulf Cooperation Council states and other U.S. regional friends, such as Jordan and Egypt, to contribute to Gulf defense. The analysis suggests that, at least for the next several years, the conventional military balance will remain favorable to the United States, as long as we continue to devote significant military resources to the region. However, barring a fundamental change in the geopolitical orientation and strategic intentions of Iraq and Iran (under current or possibly future regimes), a convergence of trends in the latter part of the decade could upset this balance.

Chapter five looks at how U.S. military requirements and force planning for the region will be affected by changes in American global defense strategy and transformation priorities. The discussion highlights the important point that U.S. strategy and force posture in the Gulf run counter to the overall changes that the military is undertaking. Regardless of what happens regionally, overall defense strategy will dictate changes in how the United States deploys its forces in the region and the strategies for their employment. Bringing the U.S. military posture in the Gulf in line with overall military doctrine will entail changes that need to be thought through with regard to the politics of relations with the Gulf states. Equally important, in the mid- to long term, the advent of new technologies and operational concepts could allow the United States to redesign its peacetime presence and its reinforcement plans for the region in ways that are militarily effective and politically palatable. In particular, the creation of small, high-tech "spearhead forces" for early entry could strengthen forward defenses while offsetting the need for both a larger peacetime presence and large, inflexible reinforcement plans. The assessment concludes that moving in this direction could free up forces for other global missions that are now rigidly allocated to Gulf missions and focused solely on an old-style war against Iraq.

Chapter six offers an overview of the objectives, interests, and policies of outside powers and the challenges and opportunities that they present for U.S. regional security strategy. It focuses in particular on the stance of these countries toward U.S. military operations in the Persian Gulf and the actions they might take, such as transfer of sophisticated conventional arms or military intervention, that could upset the geopolitical status quo or balance of military forces in the region. The discussion suggests that, in light of the challenges and constraints the United States is likely to confront, it will be easier for America to achieve its goals in the Gulf if it works in partnership with other countries rather than alone, particularly in the event that the current Iraqi regime is toppled and a new Iraqi government confronts the challenge of reconstruction, maintenance of order, and modernization. Multilateral approaches to the region's security problems will require compromises that may occasionally constrain U.S. freedom of action, but the benefits of such cooperation, especially insofar as they reduce the political, diplomatic, and material burdens of U.S. engagement in the region, outweigh the costs.

The concluding chapter discusses a post-containment strategy for adapting U.S. defense planning for the Persian Gulf to changing regional conditions in the overall context of American global defense strategy. It focuses on the following questions: Does the United States have the right strategy and posture in the region given the threat environment that it is likely to face over the next decade? What changes need to be made in the American peacetime presence, basing and access arrangements, bilateral defense relationships, military operations, force planning, and peacetime engagement activities? It puts forward a modest but important agenda for change that will allow the United States to sustain its commitments at a lower cost.

Several broad themes emerge from these assessments. First, the United States will need to adopt a more comprehensive approach to the region's problems that, while advancing such other regional goals as secure access to oil and preventing the spread of weapons of mass destruction, elevates the importance of combating terrorism in shaping the U.S. peacetime military presence and security relationships with key Gulf states. Second, the United States needs to diversify its reliance on local security partners. It remains too dependent on Saudi Arabia for supporting its military engagement in the region. Spreading America's military access arrangements more broadly throughout the region will reduce the political burdens on the Saudi royal family of sustaining its American connection while minimizing the risks that Saudi internal problems will constrain U.S. freedom of action. If the United States succeeds in toppling the Saddam Husayn regime, the need for Saudi Arabia as an ally and military outpost in the region will substantially diminish, but not disappear altogether, especially if a post-Saddam regime is slow to establish and consolidate its control over the country. Third, the drastic reduction or elimination of the Iraqi threat to the region is the sine qua non for success in guaranteeing the security of the Gulf while reducing the political costs that the U.S. military presence imposes on other interests and Gulf partners.

Not everyone will agree with the judgments and recommendations of this study. Indeed, the contributors disagree among themselves on important matters of policy and implementation, in particular whether the United States should use military force to oust the Saddam Husayn regime. Moreover, on many issues, they raise more questions than they answer. This is the case, for example, on a key political paradox that permeates this volume: the need not to abandon Saudi Arabia while at the same time reducing the U.S. footprint there. There are no simple or easy solutions to this longstanding paradox. Regardless of the outcome of the Iraqi scenario, the United States will need to maintain forces in the region, and Saudi Arabia will continue to assume an important role in the American forward deployed posture. Pulling out of Saudi Arabia would send the wrong political signals to regional players and even to the political opposition in Saudi Arabia that the United States was abandoning the regime. However, as is evident throughout the study, the U.S. military presence in Saudi Arabia is having deleterious consequences for regime stability. The discussion in chapter five suggests that this circle can be squared by projected improvements in U.S. force projection capabilities and new operational concepts. But these changes will not materialize for some time. Besides, there are grounds for questioning whether shifting more of the political and military burdens of supporting U.S. military strategy to the smaller Gulf states is sustainable over the long haul. The tension between these two perspectives runs throughout several of the chapters.

As this book goes to print, it is highly likely but not yet certain that Iraq will be disarmed by the use of military force. Also unclear is the outlook for a post-Saddam Iraq, and the region more broadly, if war becomes the only means available to enforce UN Security Council resolutions mandating the elimination of Iraqi weapons of mass destruction. Given these uncertainties, the essays herein postulate a broad range of possible outcomes to the international community's confrontation with Saddam Husayn, but they do not offer a definitive blueprint to achieve some desired end state. Rather, the purpose of this book is to illuminate the dominant factors that will shape the post-containment regional security environment and to stimulate a more in-depth discussion of the critical issues and options that lie ahead for U.S. regional security strategy.

Chapter Two

U.S. Interests and Objectives

Joseph McMillan

For more than half a century, the United States has defined its paramount national security interest in the Persian Gulf as "maintaining the unhindered flow of oil . . . to world markets at stable prices."[1] The importance of the Gulf to the global economy remains undiminished and will only increase over the coming decades. September 11, however, starkly emphasized that energy is not the only U.S. interest in the Gulf region—or even necessarily the most important. Any strategy aimed at defeating terrorism with global reach must focus heavily on the Gulf region, where so many of the September 11 terrorists originated and so many of the ideas and attitudes that drive terrorist behavior have their roots.

The Gulf area presents not only political and military challenges to U.S. national security but conceptual challenges as well. In recent decades, the American people have come to expect national strategy, especially the use of military force, to be driven by a conjunction of vital interests and core values. But in the Persian Gulf, U.S. security relations with regional states are built not on shared values, of which there are few, but instead on shared interests, of which there are many. In fact, one of the key challenges in Gulf policy has long been how to manage the divergence between interests and values, a challenge that will only grow more difficult in the years ahead.

What are U.S. interests in the Persian Gulf, and how have they changed in the last decade and especially since September 11? What are the threats to both our interests and values, and are they inevitably in conflict with each other? How will the dynamics of the regional security environment shape U.S. security strategy in advancing those interests and values? This chapter seeks to address these questions and to frame the issues, choices, and priorities confronting U.S. policy for the region. The first section provides an overview of American interests. The next section evaluates the effectiveness of past and current U.S. policies in dealing with the many issues and challenges the United States faces in fashioning a coherent regional security strategy. The last section frames strategic objectives for the future and the key factors that will shape U.S. policy choices.

Understanding U.S Interests in the Gulf

The Terrorist Backlash

Although terrorism of global reach is a diffuse and widespread phenomenon, its geographic center of gravity lies in the Persian Gulf region and its immediate periphery. Iraq and Iran have long supported terrorist operations against citizens and interests of the United States, its European allies, and moderate Middle East states. More recently, it has become apparent that the Gulf Arab states around which U.S. strategy has been built, and whose security that strategy is designed to defend, offer some of the most fertile ground for funding and recruiting transnational terror organizations. They have also been the scene of some of these groups' most devastating attacks, including bombings in Kuwait in the 1980s, Saudi Arabia in the 1990s, and Yemen in 2000.

Since September 11, it has become evident that terrorist movements no longer affect the welfare of the American people only indirectly, by threatening our national interests abroad, but directly endanger the lives and safety of Americans at home, the protection of which is among the fundamental purposes of our constitutional government. Accordingly, the suppression of terrorism driven by an antimodern backlash—a phenomenon springing in large measure from the areas bordering the Persian Gulf—must now be considered a vital national interest. Suppressing terrorism on anything but a temporary basis, however, will require addressing the conditions that breed it. Unfortunately, despite decades of study, we still do not have a full understanding of the roots of the type of terrorism that we face today, but several points are clear.

First, although much of the blame for the climate that breeds anti-Western terrorism rests with governments that are generally friendly to the United States, dealing with this problem presents dilemmas. To be sure, repressive domestic policies, ineffective economic strategies, and failure to permit evolutionary political development have historically tended to contribute to violent and extremist behavior. Yet, for many countries, abandoning repressive practices could have unintended and undesirable consequences. In the Islamic world, there is considerable risk that the removal of intrusive security practices would allow radical movements to flourish, including those that preach antidemocratic doctrines and practice violent tactics. In addition, many friendly governments in the region are faulted (correctly) for permitting or even sanctioning vitriolic anti-American and anti-Western rhetoric in state-controlled media. Unfortunately, the granting of full freedom of expression would make such rhetoric more, not less, prevalent, at least in the near term. Moreover, the United States will face tensions among the national security requirement for diplomatic and military cooperation from these states and access to their facilities, the need to promote political and social reform by their regimes (or at least to remove the popular perception that the United States is propping them up), and the prospect that responsiveness to public opinion—good in itself—will cause these governments to restrict U.S. access and refuse the cooperation needed to succeed in the antiterrorist struggle. Finally, in considering the impact of rapid democratic reform in an area where the United States has vital interests, we would do well to keep in mind Lisa Anderson's warning that "although democracies may be stable and peace loving, democratizing states rarely are."[2]

Second, the terrorists' stated policy justifications for their actions are largely specious. The U.S. military presence in the Gulf may have catalyzed sympathy for terrorist movements acting in the name of Islam and the Arab nation, but they did not cause it. Likewise, there is a connection between the Israeli-Palestinian conflict and sympathy for anti-Western terrorism, but the causal relationship is far from simple and in any case inadequate as a comprehensive explanation. No peaceful settlement of the conflict in itself can eradicate terrorism. On the contrary, such a settlement may well worsen the problem in the short term, as those who oppose reconciliation in any form redouble their efforts to derail a peace deal or even a resumption of negotiations. Over the longer run, however, resolution of the dispute could contribute to ending terrorism and the conditions that breed it, for reasons that will be explained below.

Finally, the traditional stereotype of the terrorist as a hopeless young man from the slums has proven misleading. Recent suicide bombers have included young men from wealthy Arab families, middle-aged men with jobs, wives, and children, and even young women. The current wave of terror is no more driven by economic deprivation than were the Baader-Meinhof gang and the Red Brigades of the 1970s and 1980s. Solutions to terrorism that focus on improving economic conditions will therefore be inadequate. Instead, we would do well to consider the case, made by Francis Fukuyama a decade ago, that Islamic revivalism in general and its terrorist manifestation in particular are primarily a response to feelings of cultural humiliation—that is, the sense that the Arab-Islamic world is a culture under siege, unable to fight back within the rules of even its own social and legal norms.[3]

Political Development

These observations suggest that ending terrorism and achieving political stability in the Persian Gulf will be a task of daunting complexity. On one hand, the foregoing analysis suggests that there is little hope of success in the commonly posited approaches to attacking the roots of terrorism—introducing Western-style democracy, spending money on traditional forms of foreign aid, and solving the Arab-Israeli dispute. Yet it is also clear that the Gulf region will continue to be a breeding ground of terrorism, discontent, and war unless some way can be found to bring about the political, social, economic, and intellectual changes that would enable its people to come to terms constructively with the modern world.

Over the course of 3 centuries, Islamic societies have sought to meet the challenge presented by the West by alternately imitating and rejecting it, with neither course providing satisfaction. The results of this failure are visible throughout the Islamic world, including in Iraq and Iran. Moreover, political and social Westernization that failed when it was embraced by indigenous elites is even less likely to succeed if it is foisted upon the region by outside forces. To be successful and survivable, political reform must develop organically, adapting the region's traditional religious, political, and cultural practices to meet the realities of the modern world. The question is whether such development is possible, given that the present debate often seems to be between those who, for the sake of stability, would change nothing in the current system and the radicals who would wreck the current system rather than adapt it to modern realities.

The debate outside the region has been equally fruitless. Since September 11, the lines have been drawn between those who see the introduction of sweeping democratic reforms in countries from Saudi Arabia to Egypt to Iraq as the key to "draining the swamps" where terrorism breeds[4] and those, especially regional experts, who disparage any prospect of reform as contrary to historical experience and the realities of Islam.

In discounting the chances for political evolution, the nay-sayers are disregarding not only the clear social changes that have taken place—and that have driven political changes wherever else they have occurred—but also the processes of political reform that are clearly under way in a number of countries, including Kuwait, Jordan, Yemen, Qatar, and Bahrain.

The trend of democratization has gone furthest in Iran, where reformist candidates have repeatedly won elections at the presidential, parliamentary, and local levels against the clearly expressed wishes of the ruling clerical establishment.

Conversely, those who see rapid democratization as the key to fighting terrorism seem to ignore the fact that even these successes are a mixed blessing. Many of the candidates elected are far from friendly to U.S. interests, as in the case of Iran, or to Western concepts of pluralism and universal human rights, as in Jordan, Yemen, and Kuwait. Moreover, if liberalization brings with it a wave of mass protests and street demonstrations, it might simultaneously unleash passions that are difficult to control or to channel into productive political change. Even governments that are honestly attempting to reflect the desires of their people may find themselves pushed aside by revolutionary dynamics, with dire consequences for the people of the region as well as for American interests. Those who do hang on to power would be hard pressed to support contentious U.S. policies while Washington asks them to sign what they will see as their institutional death warrants.

Even with the changes that have taken place, it is nevertheless undeniable that few Middle East political systems have kept pace with the revolution in political communication and the mobilization of opinion that have swept the region in the last 20 years. Beyond these difficult political challenges, the Gulf region, as detailed in the following chapter, also faces critical economic, demographic, and social problems that pose additional obstacles to political reforms. Like the Bourbons and Romanovs before them, ruling elites have generally responded to this social transformation—and concomitant demands for political transformation—with denial, repression, or cosmetic half-measures. The Gulf states may not be heading for violent revolution because of such pressures, but they will be increasingly forced to offer greater accommodation to mainstream demands for reform.

These trends underline an important point about American interests and military presence in the Gulf. The objective of U.S. involvement in the Gulf is stability, not preservation of the status quo. The United States has no interest in the kind of stability that comes from immobility; structures that try to remain rigid and immobile are apt to find themselves swept away by the currents swirling around them. The U.S. presence in the Gulf is intended to preserve the conditions necessary to maintain the flow of oil, primarily by ensuring that no hostile power can establish hegemony over the region. It is not designed to shield regional regimes—however friendly to our interests—from having to deal constructively with the implications of a changing world. The dilemma for the United States, of course, is that it will be accused of imperialism if it pressures regional governments to make democratic reforms and improve their human rights performance. But if it does not apply such pressure, it will be criticized for propping up regimes that are seen by their opponents as corrupt and oppressive.

In sum, the massive disruption of a revolutionary explosion would be the most dangerous outcome for the inhabitants of the region, the interests of the United States and the West, and American citizens at home. The United States therefore needs to find a way to assist the people of the region in forestalling such an explosion through successful evolutionary adaptation, even as it continues to deter, dissuade, and, if necessary, defeat aggressive behavior. Imposing a Western system on a profoundly non-Western group of societies would be resented, result in governments with less legitimacy than those now in power, and thus lead to continued instability and insecurity in the long run. Instead, the United States and the Gulf Arab states should look to accomplish three broad political tasks:

■ Create breathing space for evolutionary change by promoting the resolution of regional disputes, reducing the danger from the major destabilizing threats, and moderating the perceived cultural pressure exerted by a highly visible U.S. military presence. Extreme interpretations of Islam have historically had their strongest appeal when Muslims have believed their civilization was under pressure from without, as it is today. In a globalized world, that pressure is not going away, but moving the region away from its perpetual cycle of crises might allow many Muslims to return to the more tolerant, less political ways of manifesting the faith.

■ Support effective governance by exerting control over their national territory, delivering expected social services, and generally filling the role expected of all sovereign states in the war against global terrorism. This would simultaneously enhance the legitimacy of regional states, an issue upon which most observers of the regime place much more emphasis than upon formal democracy.

■ Foster social development by quietly encouraging the emergence of diverse voices from within the Arab and Islamic world, supporting modernization of education, and related steps. The strategic aim is for the people of the region to develop an intellectual and cultural framework that has a place for cultural coexistence and peaceful interaction with the West. A winning strategy against terrorism depends on Muslims' finding a way to reshape the way they have been taught to see history—as an eternal struggle between Islam and non-Islam.

Secure Energy

Energy, historically the number-one rationale for U.S. concerns about regional security, has been joined by the suppression of terrorism and the need for sociopolitical transformation as key U.S. interests in the Persian Gulf. It has not, however, been supplanted by them.

It is often argued that shifts in the sources from which the United States obtains its oil supplies mean that we need not be so concerned about the security of the Gulf. We have, in fact, substantially increased the quantities of oil we buy from Western Hemisphere sources, yet a larger share of the total U.S. crude oil supply nevertheless came from the Gulf in 2001 than at any other time in history. Others point to the long-term tendency of supply and demand to reach price equilibrium and the relatively low price of oil in the current market, but neither of these facts should lull us into complacency. Any forecast that extrapolates current market conditions into the future assumes continuity in the environment in which the market operates. Yet historic experience, the foregoing analysis of political, economic, and social trends in the Gulf, and the panoply of threats to security in the region argue that there is a marked probability of *dis*continuities that would sharply alter present market realities.

In some ways, the very fungibility of supplies that allows markets to stabilize in normal times is what makes all consumers worldwide feel the effect of any major disruption. In the global petroleum market, supplies literally flow to wherever the price is right, with tankers carrying millions of barrels of oil diverted en route from the wellhead to the refinery in response to trades that take place daily on the floors of exchanges in Rotterdam, London, and New York. Because of this fungibility, it is almost irrelevant whether the United States is buying its oil on any given day from Nigeria, Venezuela, or Iran. Prices are driven by worldwide supply and demand; American businesses and consumers pay the market price regardless of where the oil originates. All users throughout the world would feel the interruption of supplies from any major producer.

The secondary effects of energy supply and price discontinuities are also important. In a global economy, no one is insulated from the consequences of energy disruptions or price spikes, even if the results are not felt directly. Major U.S. trading partners are far more dependent on Gulf oil than the United States. Unreliable or excessively costly energy supplies would depress demand for our exports and increase the cost of imports. If demand were suppressed, U.S. exporters, who account for more than 10 percent of gross domestic product, 20 percent of the goods the country produces, and some 12 million American jobs, would feel the results. In the case of higher prices for imports, American consumers buying everything from Japanese electronic goods to French wines would suffer the consequences.

What is therefore relevant when assessing the importance of the Gulf to the national interest is not how much oil the United States gets from the region but the extent to which the entire global economy relies on the energy that comes from this fragile part of the world. It is particularly important to understand this reality in light of the attention that has been given to the potential of hydrocarbon deposits elsewhere.

As of the end of 2001, the Persian Gulf region was estimated to hold roughly 670 billion barrels of proven crude reserves, nearly two-thirds of the world total, as well as some 35 percent of proven natural gas reserves.[5] No other region rivals this resource base. Current estimates of proven reserves in the much-discussed Caspian Basin vary dramatically, but at most it is likely to contain some 33 billion barrels, less than 5 percent of the amount in the Gulf.[6] As investment and exploration move ahead in the Caspian Basin, the size of reserves is likely to increase dramatically. Indeed, as of February 2002, the U.S. Energy Information Administration put the total of proven, probable, and possible reserves in the Caspian at some 233 billion barrels—the apparent equivalent of another Saudi Arabia. But Persian Gulf reserves are also likely to be substantially larger than those already proven. Estimates of Iraq's possible (but as yet unproven) reserves are now placed at 220 billion barrels, about the same as in the entire Caspian Basin, while Saudi Arabia may well have recoverable petroleum resources of as much as a trillion barrels.

Current and projected production levels are in any case more relevant to patterns of energy dependence than conjecture about possible additional reserves. Over the course of 2001, the Gulf countries provided a little more than 19 million barrels a day (MBD) of crude oil, about 30 percent of global crude production. The entire former Soviet Union, including not only the non-Iranian share of the Caspian Basin but also fields in northern and eastern Russia, is likely to attain less than 75 percent of the Gulf's *current* output by 2020, when the Gulf will probably be pumping nearly 40 million barrels a day—roughly one-third of forecast worldwide production and more than 60 percent of the oil moving in international trade.

The Gulf's dominance in capacity is even more striking than its dominance in current production. More significant from a strategic point of view is that the Gulf holds 91 percent of *excess* production capacity—a measure of the ability to bring additional oil to market quickly in case of disruptions. In other words, with the Gulf now producing about 19 MBD, and spare capacity outside the Gulf of less than 900,000 barrels a day, even a 5-percent cut in Gulf output could not be quickly replaced from elsewhere. Moreover, with demand in the former Soviet Union and the developing world growing, virtually all excess production capacity will be concentrated in the Gulf within the next 2 decades.

This is not to disparage the importance of developing new sources of oil. The strategic importance of the Persian Gulf would decline geometrically if the share of global energy demand met by non-Gulf resources—or, better yet, by non-hydrocarbon resources—were to increase.[7] Unfortunately, nothing on the horizon is likely to achieve such a result to the degree that the United States and its allies can stop worrying about the security of Persian Gulf oil. Any reasonable projection shows that energy dependence on the Gulf will actually increase substantially over the next 2 decades. With global petroleum requirements expected to rise at least 50 percent over the next 20 years, only the Persian Gulf states have both the reserves and the production capacity to satisfy much of the incremental demand. Moreover, the Gulf's extraordinarily cheap production costs—less than $1.50 a barrel—and the minimal capital requirements to increase capacity there point to increasingly greater economic dependence on Gulf oil.

It is frequently argued that despite the West's dependence on oil from the Gulf, supplies are not really at risk because no supplier in the region has any choice but to pump and sell its oil—after all, as the saying goes, they cannot drink it. Even if there were a temporary disruption, the United States could ride it out with the Strategic Petroleum Reserve and similar stockpiles throughout the oil-importing world. There are, however, four serious flaws in this analysis:

- It assumes that governments will behave according to our ideas of economic rationality, as though the material welfare of their constituents (whether all the people or a small group) is uppermost on their agendas. This has not always been the case in the past, and it will not necessarily be so in the future.
- It ignores the potential effects of military aggression—not only attacks on oil facilities and transportation routes themselves but also the disruptions in the production process that are inevitable in a

wartime situation. This risk is even more salient with the growing threat from weapons of mass destruction. It also assumes that a country such as Iraq would view the economic needs of an occupied country—like Kuwait—the same way it views its own. Had the 1990 Iraqi invasion of Kuwait been allowed to stand, Saddam could have taken Kuwaiti oil production to zero and still have realized a windfall for his own treasury from skyrocketing market prices.

■ It overlooks the consequences for oil production of disruptive regime changes. The Iranian revolution is a case in point. Iranian oil production dropped from about 5.7 MBD in 1978 to 1.8 MBD in 1980, a reduction of 68 percent. A comparable cut in current Saudi production would take some five million barrels a day off the market. True, emergency stockpiles could cover the shortfall—for perhaps 3 months. The Iranian oil industry has yet to recover fully from the effects of the revolution 23 years later.

■ It neglects the importance of price. Even if supplies were only withdrawn for a short period, the ripple effect of highly unstable prices for the key commodity in the global economy could be heavily damaging and long lasting.

In summary, then, Persian Gulf petroleum resources are, and will be for the foreseeable future, a vital factor in the economic health of the United States and the world. That alone would give the Gulf region particular salience in how the U.S. Government and its armed forces shape their global strategy.

Freedom of Navigation

Not only must production and stable prices be sustained, but there also must be assurances that the oil produced can get to market. The Arabian Peninsula is bounded by three of the most important maritime chokepoints in the world—the Strait of Hormuz, the Bab el Mandeb, and the Suez Canal. (See map inside front cover.) Ninety percent of the petroleum exported from the Persian Gulf in 2000 transited the Strait of Hormuz, two-fifths of all the oil traded internationally in the world. By 2020, this flow is expected to more than double. In the near term, there is no way to offset the closure of the Strait by turning to other transportation means. Pipelines and trucks simply do not have the capacity to make up a flow of the scale that goes through the Strait.[8]

The closure of the Bab el Mandeb or Suez Canal would also cause substantial disruptions to energy trade between the Gulf and the West, although not the catastrophic disruptions that would stem from long-term closure of the Strait of Hormuz. The additional time and distance incurred in going around the Cape of Good Hope would require putting into service the equivalent of at least 30 additional very large crude carriers—a number roughly comparable to the entire tanker fleet of Exxon Mobil or Royal Dutch Shell—to maintain the current flow of oil from the Gulf to Europe.

Tankers are not the only traffic passing through the Strait of Hormuz, the Bab el Mandeb, and the Suez Canal. Apart from oil and other commercial traffic, these waterways and the airways above them play a key role in the ability of the United States to swing heavily tasked military forces from one theater to another in response to emerging and unexpected crises. Furthermore, the logistic problem of deploying and supporting forces in the Indian Ocean—as in the current operations in Afghanistan—is several times more demanding if supplies have to flow around the Cape of Good Hope or across the Pacific than if the Suez Canal and the Bab el Mandeb are available.

Of course, the United States is unlikely to lose access to these key transportation routes for any length of time under present political and military conditions. Nevertheless, a strategy toward the Gulf region must look out over a period of years. Use of the Suez Canal always depends on the inclinations of the government in Cairo; a future Egyptian regime hostile to the United States or the West could close the canal and deny U.S. flights through Egyptian airspace, thereby limiting U.S. regional military capabilities. Likewise, while the presence of a robust U.S. military force obviously limits the ability of potential aggressors to close the Strait of Hormuz or Bab el Mandeb, a reduction in the American military presence would raise the risk of a closure, depending on the attitudes of the states abutting these waterways and the capabilities of U.S. regional partners to keep them open. Even with the current level of U.S. presence, several countries, including Iran, would be able to interfere with shipping with mines, submarines, and antiship cruise missiles. As was demonstrated when the U.S. Navy had to clear Libyan mines from the Red Sea in the 1980s, it does not take a sustained effort to create a sustained disruption in traffic. The so-called tanker war between Iran and Iraq in the 1980s also showed the difficulty and danger involved in maintaining the flow of merchant traffic through a war zone, even though in that case neither combatant made a determined effort to cut off shipping completely and the impact on oil prices was minimal. In short, keeping sealanes open may be a manageable task, but it is not one that can be taken lightly.

Weapons of Mass Destruction

As the war against al Qaeda and the Taliban has made clear, U.S. interests and the threats to them do not break down into neat geographic boundaries. The effects of the endemic instability and violence that have long characterized the Middle East are no longer confined to the Middle East itself. It is thus insufficient to ask, as we might have done 10 years ago, "What U.S. interests are at risk in the Gulf?" We must now also consider the increasing threat that this cauldron of conflict presents to American friends and allies on the region's fringes and beyond.

Apart from terrorism, the most serious transregional danger emanating from the Gulf region is the continuing proliferation of weapons of mass destruction (WMD) and long-range ballistic missiles. Several of the countries of greatest concern to the United States as WMD proliferators—Iraq, Iran, Syria, and Pakistan—are either in the Gulf or on its periphery, and several other countries are at risk of following the same path. In many cases, potential targets of immediate concern to U.S. security are within range of the ballistic missiles of at least half a dozen regional powers. For example, as highlighted in chapter four, a nuclear- and missile-armed Iraq and Iran would be a threat not only to their immediate neighbors and U.S. forces operating in the Gulf but also to Israel and U.S. allies in Europe, especially Turkey.

The combination of regional dynamics and the evolution of WMD technology is apt to make such proliferation an ever-accelerating and increasingly destabilizing phenomenon over the next decade, enormously complicating the development and execution of U.S. policy. In the first place, there are no strategic dyads in the Middle East—nothing comparable to the relationship that led to stalemate in the U.S.-Soviet strategic struggle during the Cold War. Even if a particular country sees its own WMD programs as aimed against a single particular enemy, other regional and even extraregional states will not perceive it that way and will react to the perceived threat accordingly. As a result, the so-called security dilemma is likely to come into play with a vengeance, as country A's efforts to enhance its own security vis-à-vis country B are quickly offset by unexpected countermoves on the part of countries C, D, and E. Clearly, this is a formula for a strategic arms race of major proportions.[9]

Moreover, advances in WMD technology, particularly in the development of new biological and chemical agents and unconventional means for delivering them, will vastly complicate the defensive aspects of any counterproliferation strategy. It will therefore become increasingly difficult for the United States to persuade regional states that it will be able to defend them from attack if their support for U.S. policy puts them at risk. This could have two possible effects, neither of them positive. On the one hand, weaker states could decide that siding with the United States is what makes them targets; the way to avoid being attacked with weapons of mass destruction may be to avoid giving the possessors of the weapons reason to attack. Conversely, those who are able to do so may decide that they have no choice but to acquire deterrent capabilities of their own, further destabilizing an already unstable balance. Given the passions that divide the region and the long history of disastrous decisionmaking, such a prospect can only be described as bleak.[10]

Evaluating the Strategic Record

Many of the challenges facing the United States in the Gulf today were explicitly discussed in May 1993, when the Clinton administration unveiled its dual containment strategy. This approach to regional security, which has governed U.S. Gulf policy for most of the ensuing years, was explicitly founded on four basic premises:

- Both Iraq and Iran were hostile to American interests in the Middle East and, implicitly, were likely to remain so for the indefinite future.
- Iran presented the more serious threat.
- Seeking regional security by balancing Iraq and Iran against each other would be ineffective, dangerous, and unnecessary.
- The Gulf War coalition could be sustained to defend the region against the threats posed by both countries.

A fifth premise, unstated in public, was that the turmoil in Iraq after the Gulf War and the reign of terror necessary to suppress it underscored the weakness of Saddam Husayn's regime. The strategy, then, was to place this weak regime on the horns of a dilemma. If Saddam humiliated Iraq by fully implementing the post-Gulf War cease-fire resolutions, his own generals would oust him; if he did not, the prolonged application of sweeping economic sanctions would lead to a wave of popular unrest that would topple the regime.

Nevertheless, although expressing a strong preference for a change of regime in Baghdad, the first Clinton administration did not make it an overt part of its policy. Instead, the United States would follow a strategy of enhanced containment comprising three elements:

- demanding compliance with United Nations (UN) Security Council resolutions[11]
- providing humanitarian support to the Iraqi people
- ensuring, through the UN resolutions and their enforcement and inspection measures, that as long as the Saddam Husayn regime survives, it will not be in a position to threaten its neighbors or to suppress its people with impunity.

The administration characterized the challenge facing the United States from Iran as more difficult. Tehran's hostile intentions were not subsiding, and its capabilities were increasing. Moreover, the existence of international sanctions against Iraq but not Iran was dangerously shifting the regional balance in favor of Iran.[12] In response, the Clinton administration adopted a policy called active containment (to differentiate it from the Iraq policy of enhanced containment). While the United States would not seek a confrontation with Iran, neither would it normalize relations until Iran changed its objectionable policies with respect to WMD, support for international terrorism, and opposition to the peace process. Although it would be open to dialogue conducted through authoritative (that is, official) channels, the United States would work to block Iranian acquisition of both WMD and threatening conventional weapons and to isolate Iran economically until it saw significant changes in Iranian behavior.

In retrospect, much can be said in favor of the Clinton administration 1993 Middle East policy. It clearly linked the Arab-Israeli peace process to U.S. interests in the Gulf, and it identified pressure for social and political change as a key source of violence for the future—a prescient statement seen from the perspective of September 11, 2001. Yet the Clinton administration policy toward the Gulf was largely unsuccessful, mainly because two of the key assumptions on which it was built turned out to be badly flawed, although they seemed altogether reasonable at the time.

Iraq: Unexpected Stasis

Given the devastation of two major wars in the space of 10 years, a crippled economy, crushing international debt, 2 widespread rebellions, foreign occupation and overflight of substantial portions of the country, and sweeping UN sanctions, few analysts looking at Iraq in the early 1990s would have given Saddam Husayn much chance of surviving into the 21st century. Yet the Iraqi regime turned out to be more durable and resilient than most people thought. As the post-Gulf War stalemate with Baghdad stretched into its seventh and eighth years, both the coalition and the international consensus on sanctions began to unravel. Over the second half of the 1990s, it became apparent that containment exercised through sanctions, inspections, and no-fly zones could not bring about regime change, secure Iraqi compliance with its cease-fire commitments, or provide any degree of certainty that Iraq was not developing WMD. Saddam succeeded in making the United States, rather than his own recalcitrance, appear responsible for the suffering of Iraqis under sanctions. The United States was forced to accept increasingly looser interpretations of the term *food* and progressively higher ceilings on the amount of Iraqi oil that could be exported under the oil-for-food program. As a result, Iraq was able to export legally all the oil it could produce and import virtually any kind of consumer good on the market. Increasingly, the UN-based strategy that had been a key source of legitimacy when the United States had clear international support now became a liability.

Meanwhile, as other crises demanded attention, the mood in the administration began to shift against the desirability of confrontation. In particular, following Secretary General Kofi Annan's compromise that headed off a confrontation over the UN Special Commission access to Iraqi presidential sites in February 1998, the Clinton administration concluded that reacting to Iraqi provocations actually strengthened rather than weakened Saddam's position. Accordingly, it began looking for ways to move Iraq off the front pages and avoid incidents that would require the use of force. Nevertheless, Saddam Husayn's persistence in testing the limits of obstruction eventually forced the Clinton administration to launch the most robust coalition military action since the Gulf War, the four days of missile and air attacks known as *Desert Fox*. By that time, however, it had already become obvious that using sanctions, inspections, and the threat of military retaliation to contain the Iraqi regime, let alone to create the conditions leading to Saddam's ouster, was a strategy whose time had passed. It was time to choose one of two options: take more direct action to bring about a change of regime and the forcible resolution of the Iraq problem, or retrench into long-term deterrence and containment. Under the latter approach, the United States, as it has done on the Korean Peninsula, would accept the continued survival of a hostile regime in a vital region but defend against Iraq with a robust forward presence and deter it from egregious conduct with the threat of overwhelming retaliation.

Faced with these alternatives, the administration half-heartedly chose a combination of both options with a policy it labeled *containment plus regime change*.[13] Driven by Congressional enactment of the Iraq

Liberation Act, the Clinton administration made regime change an explicit part of its policy in late 1998,[14] although with serious reservations. At the same time, the administration set forth a set of red lines characteristic of a strategy of deterrence and containment, but phrased in a way that left considerable doubt whether the United States would actually use force if the red lines were crossed.[15] Finally, the administration put considerable diplomatic effort into reconstructing a WMD inspection regime, offering relaxation of sanctions in return for Iraqi cooperation. Yet it did not include Iraqi rejection of the Security Council resolution setting up the new monitoring commission among the red lines for use of force. In fact, Secretary of State Madeleine Albright explicitly ruled out use of force for that purpose.[16]

In some respects, stating regime change as an overt goal made dealing with the Iraq question more difficult. It definitely changed the metric by which U.S. actions vis-à-vis Iraq were measured, to the detriment of American credibility. The case of the new Operation *Southern Watch* response options illustrated this conundrum. In response to stepped-up Iraqi challenges to the no-fly zones following *Desert Fox*, the U.S. Central Command was given flexibility to strike targets related to air defense in southern Iraq. The use of this authority seriously degraded Iraqi air defense capabilities in the south and left coalition forces in an enhanced position to conduct additional operations on short notice if directed. Furthermore, by permitting verification and enforcement of UN Security Council (UNSC) Resolution 949—which bans the enhancement of Iraqi forces in the southern part of the country—*Southern Watch* makes a direct contribution to the coalition's ability to defend Kuwait. Yet the adoption of more assertive ground rules for this operation has been repeatedly faulted because it has not decisively undermined the regime—even though it was not designed for that purpose nor, given British reservations about regime change as a legitimate policy objective, could it have done so without unraveling the last remnants of the *Desert Storm* coalition.

The fact that all U.S. actions were now examined in light of their contribution to a declaratory policy of regime change also accelerated the erosion of international consensus. Governments that were comfortable with securing the region against renewed Iraqi aggression, limiting Iraqi military capabilities, and enforcing compliance with UN resolutions were less willing to sign up to overthrow the recognized government of Iraq. With regime change front and center, the rest of our agenda became suspect. Governments that would have been inclined to support U.S. policy on everything *except* regime change found it difficult to support *any* aspect of U.S. policy once regime change came to be seen as the ultimate end of the policy as a whole. Even those who would have been more than willing to support the covert overthrow of the Ba´thists found that without the cover of plausible deniability they were no longer able to do so.

Shortly after coming into office, the Bush administration tried to salvage what was left of sanctions by pursuing Security Council endorsement of what have been called smart sanctions. These would narrow the range of prohibited goods to a well-defined list of items that would make a clear contribution to military capabilities. They would also partially shift responsibility for enforcing prohibitions from member states (that is, the United States) to the UN bureaucracy. Finally, they would tighten controls on oil smuggling by enlisting the support of Iraq's neighbors. In effect, this approach sought to make the best of a bad situation, retrenching from a position that was no longer diplomatically tenable. Conceptually, the idea had merit. In practice, it was dead on arrival, given the unyielding Iraqi opposition to anything that might legitimate the continuation of sanctions. In any case, the other key element of the smart sanctions proposal—the expectation that the countries providing the principal avenues for smuggling could be persuaded to crack down on the illicit traffic in defiance of their own economic and political interests—proved totally unrealistic.

Iran: Unexpected Change

In contrast, Iran was more susceptible to change within the framework of the Islamic Revolution than anyone thought possible in 1993. By 2000, it was obvious that the tide of opinion in Iran was on the side of sweeping peaceful reform within the framework of the constitution, including reining in the clout of the reactionary clergy. A reformist president and parliament had been elected, social restrictions had been relaxed, and a freer press permitted. Dual containment made no allowance for any of this, or for the possibility that the United States and Iran might have convergent interests in the region that could open the way to tacit cooperation. Indeed, the passage of the Iran-Libya Sanctions Act in 2001 had the effect of hardening the U.S. position at the very time a glimmer of change was becoming visible in Iran.

For a time, the Bush administration seemed to be divided over how and whether to move forward on normalization with Iran. Advocates of a policy shift contended that sanctions harm no one but American companies and that the long-term U.S. interest is to reinforce moves toward moderation in Iran. Opponents responded that continued Iranian support for Hizballah and Palestinian terrorist groups and its pursuit of nuclear and missile capabilities—especially those that threaten Israel—demonstrate that Iran's real agenda has not changed. Supreme Leader Ali Khamenei's antagonistic comments following the September 11 attacks, a dramatic backtracking from the Mohammed Khatami government's initially sympathetic reaction, only stiffened support for containment and isolation. President Bush's labeling of Iran as part of an axis of evil, along with Iraq and North Korea, appeared to strengthen domestic opponents of an Iranian opening to the United States.

Nevertheless, it has been easier to see that, since September 11, the United States and Iran have convergent interests on certain key issues. Despite U.S. dissatisfaction with Iranian meddling in northwestern Afghanistan after the fall of the Taliban, and even in the face of the possibility that important elements in the Iranian power structure may have allowed al Qaeda operatives to take refuge in their country, Iran nevertheless has an enduring national interest in stability in Afghanistan and the ultimate suppression of the virulently anti-Shi'ite al Qaeda. U.S. and Iranian interests are also congruent on the issues of Iraq and narcotics smuggling.

There has been modest forward movement despite the rhetoric and reservations on both sides. The administration included the anti-Iranian Mujahideen al-Khalq on the new U.S. list of terrorist groups, something Tehran had been seeking for some time. In response to a U.S. request, the Iranian government agreed to the use of its territory for search and rescue operations for downed coalition aircrews in Afghanistan as well as the transshipment of U.S. food supplies to Afghanistan through Bandar Abbas. More recently, Tehran announced that any U.S. personnel downed in Iranian territory during a possible U.S. war with Iraq would be promptly repatriated. Perhaps most significantly, members of Congress, including some of Israel's most solid supporters, have met with senior Iranian officials to discuss the way ahead.

Despite these convergent interests, the path toward U.S.-Iranian reconciliation is strewn with obstacles. Most obviously, hard-liners continue to control those parts of the Iranian security apparatus responsible for the behavior that led President Bush to include Iran in the axis of evil: pursuit of weapons of mass destruction, support for international terrorist groups, and support for violent resistance to the Arab-Israeli peace process. Recent reports of the extent of covert Iranian nuclear weapons development efforts are especially troubling. Furthermore, many of the Iranian policies and practices the United States opposes enjoy broad-based domestic support from across the Iranian political spectrum. Just because Khatami wants better relations with the West does not mean that he would terminate Iran's WMD program to get them.

Looking toward a Post-September 11 Gulf

Given the Persian Gulf's inherent ability to affect the lives of Americans in quite dramatic ways, how would one go about devising a U.S. security strategy toward the region? To begin, it must be shaped by several overarching objectives.

First, the United States must limit the ability of regional forces—whether state or nonstate actors—to endanger American citizens, interests, and allies. Although U.S. interests and nationals have long been the objects of terrorist attacks and military operations in the region, September 11 demonstrated the potential for forces emanating from this region to destroy American lives and damage the welfare of the American people.

Second, the United States and its partners must prevent any single power from establishing hegemony over the Gulf. U.S. interests in the Gulf are so important that the United States and its allies must ensure they are not vulnerable to pressure or blackmail.

Third, the risk of conflict in the region must be reduced. Rivalries over succession, resources, ideology, and territory have already caused hundreds of thousands of deaths and untold economic losses. Moreover, the constant threat of external attack has served as the real or putative justification for highly repressive political structures. Persistent conflict has also contributed to the cultural feeling of being under siege, feeding the growth of terrorism. With the spread of missiles and WMD, the potential for a conflict to escalate out of control is growing yearly. The international community and region itself must find effective mechanisms for peaceful conflict resolution.

Finally, external intervention, even if stabilizing in the short term, has a corrosive effect the longer it continues. Yet simply withdrawing from the U.S. commitment to regional security would be self-defeating. Over the long run, therefore, the United States must find ways, through aid, diplomacy, and influence, to foster enduring stability through evolutionary political and economic development.

These objectives are easy to state but more difficult to attain because, in many cases, the apparent solution to one problem only aggravates others. For example, the most obvious way to ensure that the flow of oil is not endangered by the hegemonic ambitions of a hostile power is to base a robust U.S. or coalition force in the Gulf on a permanent basis. Yet doing so would fuel the anti-Western attitudes from which terrorism springs and reduce the likelihood that regional states will pursue the reforms on which long-term stability depends.

There are similar tensions between the oil importing countries' interest in low prices and our countervailing interest in the oil producing states' investing adequately in national defense. Moreover, if oil prices are low, every riyal spent on defense—including those spent to support foreign forces—is a riyal taken away from social spending, fueling public dissatisfaction with friendly regional governments. Yet money spent on social services rather than defense capabilities serves to perpetuate the need for the presence of U.S. forces, which also stirs popular disgruntlement.

Finally, Iraqi recalcitrance about living up to the cease-fire and disarmament resolutions passed by the UNSC over the past 12 years has made it necessary to keep a significant force in the Gulf to maintain limits on Iraqi forces and to enforce the sanctions regime as well as defend against renewed Iraqi aggression. Paradoxically, however, the measures required to contain the Iraqi threat have also eroded the regional consensus that containment is desirable.

Within this complex environment, U.S. success in achieving its strategic objectives in the Persian Gulf over the coming decade depends mainly on three key variables:

- how effectively the Gulf Cooperation Council (GCC) states respond to pressures for domestic change
- how Iran's political evolution plays out and is reflected in Iranian foreign policy
- whether the Iraqi regime survives and reconstitutes its hegemonic threat.

The GCC States: Evolution or Revolution?

The moderate Arab countries of the Persian Gulf region clearly are facing social and economic pressures that could transform their politics within the next decade. In addition, Saudi Arabia, Kuwait, and Oman are almost certain to undergo leadership successions, strictly on the basis of actuarial realities. There is always the possibility of illness, whether unexpected or not, claiming the lives of other leaders as well. Moreover, there are uncertainties in many of these countries as to who the next rulers will be, whether because the process of succession is unclear, the candidates for office beyond the current aging generation of rulers have not been identified, or the designated heirs' political sustainability is open to question.

On the other hand, the imminent demise of the hereditary monarchies of the Gulf has been predicted ever since the Egyptian and Iraqi armies overthrew their respective royal families in the 1950s. Moreover, while some threats to regime stability have grown in recent decades—notably the violent form of radical political Islam characterized by al Qaeda—others seem to have subsided. Ba´thism is an ideology without popular appeal, even on its home turf. Iranian efforts to subvert the Shiah populations of Saudi Arabia and Bahrain, which were extremely active immediately following the 1979 revolution, are also largely a thing of the past, a casualty of Iran's expanding ties to Riyadh, Manama, and Kuwait.

Iran: Prolonged Confrontation or Détente?

The future direction of Iran is murky. The long-term internal trends seem positive, and it is not inconceivable that the United States may some day work productively with Tehran on behalf of regional security. If that should come to pass, the United States would be able to diversify its relationships, making them less dependent on cooperation with the GCC states. More realistically, however, change in Iran may take years to play out and would be unlikely to yield a regime that is as fully responsive to U.S. blandishments and pressures as Washington might like. Moreover, any Iranian government will see itself as the dominant power in the Gulf, while any U.S. administration that learned the lessons of the 1980s will be loathe to entrust the Iranians with that role. Thus, even under optimal conditions, there will be tensions between Washington and Tehran over the structure of regional security, and conditions are likely to be far less than optimal as Iran continues pursuing the acquisition of nuclear weapons, other WMD, and long-range missiles. In short, political evolution in Iran very likely will eventually allow the United States to adjust its commitments and deployments in the Gulf but not to shed them altogether, at least not soon.

Given the history of the U.S.-Iranian relationship since 1979, American ability to influence how developments unfold in Iran is bound to be modest. That history also suggests that either obvious support for reform or steadfast hostility to the regime is apt to be detrimental to liberalization and moderation. Even apart from Iran's internal political dynamics, however, the United States faces important strategic decisions on how to deal with this traditionally most powerful of Gulf states. As already noted, the United States and Iran have both contradictory and complementary interests. The administration must therefore decide not between resolutely condemning or wholeheartedly embracing Iran, but whether seizing opportunities for tactical cooperation on discrete issues, such as Iraq and Afghanistan, is necessarily incompatible with maintaining pressure on other issues, such as terrorism and WMD. In other words, can and should the United States develop the kind of relationship with Iran that it maintains with other countries, such as China, with whom simultaneous cooperation and conflict are the norm?

In any case, Iran should not be seen as the major determinant of U.S. military presence in the Gulf region—especially non-naval presence— under foreseeable circumstances. It is true, as discussed in chapter four, that Iran has been significantly upgrading its military capabilities in the past several years, but primarily in the areas of naval forces, air defense, and ballistic missiles. Iran has no plausible way of bringing land force to bear against the GCC states, other than in such limited ways as it has used on Abu Musa and the Greater and Lesser Tunbs, the islands whose ownership it disputes with the United Arab Emirates. Its amphibious warfare capability is extremely limited, while the Iraqi Army, even in its currently reduced state, blocks an attack overland.

Iran could more seriously challenge U.S. interests through terrorism and renewed support for subversion; through acquisition or threat to use WMD; or by attempting to interfere with the seaborne movement of naval forces or commerce. In a wartime situation, it could mount airstrikes against petroleum infrastructure in the eastern parts of Saudi Arabia or missile attacks against shipping in the Gulf. The Gulf Arab states are quite capable of dealing with the possibility of airstrikes, and the U.S. Navy can easily handle any attempt to close the sealanes. Otherwise, none of the other threats would require the presence of significant U.S. land-based forces, with the possible exception of relatively small, low-visibility missile defense units. This is not to say that the Iranian WMD threat is negligible or that it will not change the security dynamic of the Persian Gulf in very substantial ways. But the nature of the dangers posed by Iran is such that they cannot be countered merely by the physical presence of conventional forces in close geographic proximity. They certainly would not require a presence beyond that already required to deter an Iraqi invasion of Kuwait.

Whither Iraq?

Of the three variables, the future of Saddam Husayn's Iraq will have the greatest short-term impact on the U.S. military presence. As long as Iraq threatens American interests in the Gulf, the United States has little choice but to maintain the capability to deter or defeat that threat with a combination of in-theater and rapidly deployable forces. Baghdad's refusal to comply with the requirements of the cease-fire that ended the 1990–1991 Gulf War, and the Clinton administration decision to deal with this refusal primarily through a policy of containment, drove the United States to eschew a more sustainable concept of Gulf security at reduced levels of presence, as was envisioned immediately after the war.

At least as long as Saddam remains in power, the U.S. military footprint in the Gulf must therefore be determined by the military concept of operations for the region's defense against Iraq. Without a presence along approximately existing lines, prepared and capable of responding immediately to any Iraqi force movement well before an actual invasion, forward defense of Kuwait is impracticable. Moreover, the forces that have been maintained in place since the late 1990s make it possible to respond rapidly to other Iraqi provocations or to transition quickly to offensive operations if the President decides to do so. Maintaining a robust force in the region and sustaining its pattern of military operations are of immeasurable value in being able to execute such a plan on short notice. The use of the no-fly zones to keep Iraqi air defenses suppressed is particularly valuable because it allows the early stages of a major operation to be compressed by at least 48 to 72 hours. One lesson of the past decade is that opportunities to damage the Iraqi regime must be seized quickly when they present themselves; otherwise, diplomatic actions to alleviate tensions—by negotiating a compromise between Iraq's desires and its existing international commitments—tend to move more quickly than the diplomatic and military actions necessary to enforce those commitments. Iraq's proclivity for "cheating and retreating" and its ability to draw the international community into extended negotiations—a proclivity being played out anew in the game of cat and mouse Baghdad is playing with the UN Monitoring, Verification, and Inspection Commission (UNMOVIC)—demonstrate that it is crucial to be able to act rapidly if one is to act at all.

The assured capability of applying overwhelming U.S. force on short notice is therefore crucial to any undertaking to oust the Iraqi regime. The Bush administration is well on its way to assembling that capability and may finally have succeeded in crafting the diplomatic trap for Baghdad that will enable the United States to act when the time comes. If it does so, the attempt must not only be quick; it must also be decisive.

Any attempt at regime change—especially one overtly backed by the United States—cannot be permitted to fail. The attempt itself will inevitably cause diplomatic damage, but the damage can probably be re-paired if the attempt succeeds. If it fails, the damage will be so serious that there will be no second chance. The United States must also have a credible plan for managing the post-conflict phase of regime change that could require a sustained, expensive, and politically risky commitment to nation-building and regime protection, as well as a prolonged com-mitment of U.S. forces to a multinational occupation force.

What if the United States ultimately elects not to proceed with im-posing regime change in Iraq? The rationale for such a decision would pre-sumably be that the Iraqi threat is limited and manageable for the foresee-able future under some kind of UN-brokered compromise and that the likely costs to the United States—in human, economic, and political terms—would exceed the benefits gained by ousting the regime.

Undertaking regime change in Iraq would clearly draw the United States into a much more ambitious involvement in Iraqi affairs over a much longer period than most Americans would wish. Considering the damage done by decades of Saddam Husayn's rule, the challenges of build-ing a minimally humane state, let alone a democracy, are staggering. The prospects for full success may well be even slimmer than elsewhere in the region. At best, a new government imposed by the United States will face major hurdles in terms of popular and regional legitimacy.

Nevertheless, imposed regime change seems the least bad of the ap-parent choices. The most obvious alternative, long-term containment, must confront the reality that sanctions will soon be all but impossible to enforce. It is widely suggested that Iraqi cooperation with UN weapons monitors can safely be traded for the dropping of economic sanctions. Surely the lesson of the UN Special Commission (UNSCOM) is that no in-spection regime can provide an acceptable degree of certainty that Iraq is abiding by its obligations to forgo WMD. For 7 years, the only way UNSCOM ever got anything approaching acceptable access was at the point of American guns. There is no basis for believing things will be dif-ferent for UNMOVIC.

Long-term containment would therefore look much more like con-tainment of North Korea than the approach that was used with Iraq in the early to mid-1990s. Replicating the Korean approach in the Persian Gulf, however, seems highly problematic. In the first place, doing so would gen-erate even greater popular resentment in the region, both against the United States and friendly countries whose security we are trying to en-sure. In the Far East, the United States maintains a forward presence of roughly 100,000 personnel devoted primarily to the North Korean threat, notwithstanding that the South Korean armed forces alone match up far more credibly against North Korea than the GCC states would against Iraq. To maintain long-term containment of Iraq under circumstances in which sanctions had eroded, Iraqi capabilities were being rebuilt, and the consensus that now permits intrusive U.S. air operations in peacetime had vanished would require a U.S. peacetime presence on the order of 50,000. The problems surrounding the U.S. military presence in Korea and Okinawa would pale in comparison with those that would result from an open-ended U.S. presence of this size in the much more xeno-phobic and less populous Persian Gulf. Even from a purely geographic point of view, Kuwait is ill-suited to the role of South Korea, with less than one-quarter the land area and less than half the strategic depth. An even more crucial question is whether the American public and Congress would be prepared to support an ongoing commitment on this scale, par-ticularly if they perceived that the people most immediately affected by the threat—the inhabitants of the region—were hostile to the United States and to American military personnel.

Another possibility would be to accept Iraq's reconstitution as a major regional threat, perhaps this time with nuclear weapons and delivery means, and to rely on the threat of overwhelming retaliation to deter Iraqi adventurism. The apparent success of this strategy in deterring Saddam Husayn from using chemical weapons in 1991 may suggest that such a pol-icy can succeed again, but assuming that it would work again is fraught with risk, particularly in light of Saddam's track record of miscalculating U.S. options, intentions, and capabilities. Both North Korea's likely posses-sion of one or two nuclear weapons and its conventional military capabili-ties have deterred the Bush administration from using military force to eliminate Pyongyang's nuclear program. Indeed, these facts are a sobering reminder of how Iraq's possession of nuclear weapons might alter the future geostrategic landscape in the Gulf.

Conclusion

America's historic interests in the Gulf were unaltered by the events of September 11. If anything, the terrorist attacks demonstrated that con-ditions and events in the Gulf, and in the wider Middle East, are of even more immediate importance to the security and safety of the American people than we realized on September 10. It is that lesson that should lead the U.S. Government to begin taking the difficult actions necessary for the long-term, orderly evolution of the Gulf and its security environment. Of particular importance is the reduction of the standing American military presence. Ultimately, that presence cannot and need not go to zero, or even return to the modest level of the era before the Iraqi invasion of Kuwait. But it does need to be less visible, and less seemingly permanent, than it is today—an option that might become more militarily feasible in the future, as suggested in chapter five, as U.S. Armed Forces incorporate new technologies and operational concepts, and if Saddam is removed from power. Yet making any far-reaching reductions in the U.S. military presence absent offsetting enhancements would be imprudent—even reckless—as long as a hostile Iraqi regime remains in power and the promise of transformation is years away from reaching fruition. Indeed, the survival of the Iraqi regime would make it just as necessary to maintain a robust U.S. military presence in the near term as it is to reduce that presence in the long term. The only safe way to reduce U.S. forces is after Saddam's regime is destroyed and his WMD programs are eliminated.

Notes

[1] Department of Defense, Office of International Security Affairs, *United States Security Strategy for the Middle East* (Washington, DC: Department of Defense, May 1995), 6.

[2] Lisa Anderson, "Arab Democracy: Dismal Prospects," *World Policy Journal* 18, no. 3 (Fall 2001), 53–60.

[3] Francis Fukuyama, *The End of History and the Last Man* (New York: Free Press, 1992), 162–173, 237.

[4] See, for instance, such diverse sources as President Clinton's October 6, 2001, speech at Yale University, accessed at <http://www.yale.edu/opa/news/clinton.html>; Benjamin R. Barber, "Beyond Jihad vs. McWorld," *The Nation* 274, no. 2 (January 21, 2002), 11–18; and Robert Kagan and William Kristol, "The Bush Doctrine Unfolds," *Weekly Standard*, March 4, 2002, 11.

[5] Energy Information Administration, *International Energy Outlook 2002*, Report No. DOE/EIA–0484 (Washington, DC: Department of Energy, 2002).

[6] Energy Information Administration fact sheet, "Caspian Sea Region," February 2002.

[7] However, any benefit from a shift to Caspian sources would be undermined to the extent that production flowed by pipeline to the Gulf and then out the Strait of Hormuz. This is all but inevitable for at least the Iranian share of Caspian Basin production.

[8] The Center for Strategic and International Studies puts transpeninsular pipeline capacity at roughly seven MBD. See its report "Strategic Energy Initiative: Task Force Report on the Middle East" (1998), accessed at <http://www.csis.org/sei/work/Metfreport.html>.

[9] The author uses the term *strategic* to mean as viewed by the regional states themselves, not necessarily as constituting an existential threat to the United States itself.

[10] For a detailed exposition of these issues, see Steven L. Spiegel, "Arms Control: In the Region's Future?" in *The Middle East in 2015*, ed. Judith S. Yaphe (Washington, DC: National Defense University Press, 2002), 195–212.

[11] This was to be the top priority: "It should be clear that we seek full compliance for all Iraqi regimes," Martin S. Indyk said. "We will not be satisfied with Saddam's overthrow before we agree to lift sanctions. Rather, we will want to be satisfied that any successor government complies fully with all UN resolutions."

[12] The inconsistency between this concern and the administration's denial that it intended Iraq and Iran to balance one another seems to have gone unremarked.

[13] Or, as it was subsequently and less boldly stated, "containment until regime change."

[14] "Saddam's actions over the past decade make clear that his regime will not comply with its obligations under the UN Security Council resolutions designed to rid Iraq of WMD and their delivery systems. Because of that and because the Iraqi people will never be free under the brutal dictatorship of Saddam Hussein, we actively support those who seek to bring a new democratic government to power in Baghdad. We recognize that this may be a slow and difficult process, but we believe it is the only solution to the problem of Saddam's regime." See *National Security Strategy for a New Century*, December 1999.

[15] The standard statement of these red lines was: "We currently maintain a credible force in the region and are prepared to act at an appropriate time and place of our choosing if Iraq reconstitutes its weapons of mass destruction programs, threatens its neighbors or U.S. forces, or moves against the Kurds." This sentiment was most recently repeated by Assistant Secretary of State Edward S. Walker, Jr., testimony before the Senate Armed Services Committee, September 19, 2000, accessed at <http://usinfo.state.gov/regional/nea/iraq/walker919.htm>.

[16] Barbara Crossette and Steven Lee Myers, "U.S. Forswears Force Over Iraq Inspections," *The New York Times*, September 13, 2000, 1.

Chapter Three

Gulf Security Perceptions and Strategies

Judith S. Yaphe

The interests and security policies of the governments in the Persian Gulf—from the so-called pariah states of Iraq and Iran to Yemen and the six countries that comprise the Gulf Cooperation Council (GCC)—have long been intertwined with those of the United States.[1] Wars, border disputes, success and collapse of the Arab-Israeli peace process, and recurring instability in the international oil market have posed grave concerns for the well-being of the region as well as the United States, but these developments are no longer the main drivers of regional or U.S. strategy and defense policy. The key security issues that shape American policy in the Gulf today include eliminating Iraq as a threat to the security and stability of the region, maintaining support for the war on terrorism, securing access to reasonably priced oil, and preventing Iran from acquiring weapons of mass destruction (WMD) or taking actions that are hostile to U.S. interests.

Dual containment as an effective and enforceable policy has run its course. For the GCC states, the priorities are different from those of the United States, and the influences affecting their security and defense policies are different, too. U.S. policy and operations in the region—including the defeat of Iraq, the liberation of Kuwait, and the successes of the United Nations Special Commission (UNSCOM) inspectors—achieved impressive results, but the United States may also be a victim of its own success in the way the GCC states have reacted to these developments. Thirteen years after Iraq invaded and occupied Kuwait and 24 years after the Iranian revolution, which threatened to disrupt the Gulf by exporting its revolution, most Gulf governments would prefer to restore the balance-of-power system in the Gulf as it existed more or less before August 2, 1990. This chapter examines the factors shaping how these governments formulate their security and defense policies.

The Gulf Arab Security Vision, Then and Now

Since the early 1960s, Saudi Arabia, Kuwait, Bahrain, Qatar, the United Arab Emirates (UAE), and Oman have preferred (or, better yet, allowed) outsiders to define their security policies and needs. New to acting like states rather than tribes, but not yet wealthy from oil and accustomed to letting tradition determine their governance and institutions of civil society, the smaller Arab states of the Persian Gulf initially followed their colonial protector, Great Britain, to shelter themselves from the Arab and Persian nationalist storms that periodically swept through the neighborhood. The exception was Saudi Arabia, which enjoyed better relations with the United States than with the United Kingdom. Iran under the Shah and Iraq under kings, military dictators, and a Ba´thist republic alternately stormed through the Gulf threatening to retake Kuwait and Bahrain and seize islands and oilfields in the Gulf itself. When the British decided that they could no longer afford to protect the Gulf Arabs and withdrew in 1971, the smaller and fragile Gulf states turned to the United States to assume the British mantle.

Through the 1970s and 1980s, the Arab states of the Gulf faced the hegemonic ambitions of Iran, first under the secular and intensely nationalistic regime of the Shah and then under the revolutionary Islamic Republic of Iran, determined to export its revolution across the Gulf. In between Iranian challenges came Iraqi feints at territorial acquisition, as well as attempts to gain influence in decisionmaking on Gulf and wider Arab political, economic, and strategic affairs. After the British withdrawal east of Suez and concerned about possible Soviet encroachments in the Gulf, President Richard Nixon created the Twin Pillars policy, which designated Iran and Saudi Arabia as proxies for U.S. military presence in the region.[2] With the fall of the Shah in 1979, the United States increased its presence and role in the Gulf. In November 1979, the Carter administration defined the Gulf as vital to U.S. interests and established the Rapid Deployment Joint Task Force as the principal tool for its defense.[3]

U.S. military involvement increased dramatically during the Iran-Iraq War when the United States permitted the reflagging of Kuwaiti-owned commercial vessels under the American flag, entitling them to U.S. Navy protection against Iranian attacks (Operation *Earnest Will*). When it seemed that Tehran might succeed in defeating Baghdad and thus increase its ability to subvert the smaller Gulf states, the United States provided limited assistance to Baghdad. It was still a policy of balance of power, with Baghdad now the short-term "protector." The U.S. presence was still considered to be offshore and over the horizon, with no bases or homeporting rights, except for

Bahrain and Oman, where access agreements had been established to allow prepositioning of military equipment. The GCC was formed in 1981 as a means of self-protection against Iraq and Iran. Although protection from the war may have been on their minds, in reality GCC leaders from the outset used the council primarily as a sounding board for regional security issues and cooperation on economic policy.

The Iraqi invasion of Kuwait shattered the myth of U.S. over-the-horizon presence and exposed the Arabs to their inability to prevent their large, powerful, and angry neighbors—now Iraq, then Iran—from taking out their wrath or seeking succor in the oilfields of Kuwait and the Gulf at large. Also, to the relief of the rulers and the concern of the ruled, it brought the U.S. military into the region with a reshaped strategic doctrine and security perceptions. For a while after the war, it seemed as if the United States would maintain a significant military footprint and the GCC would stay under an American security umbrella to protect the regimes, their oil, and sealanes from hegemonic threats from Iraq or Iran. The GCC states were especially supportive of UNSCOM efforts to detect, inspect, and destroy Iraqi nuclear, biological, and chemical (NBC) capabilities and were disturbed by its demise in 1998.

Good feelings about the U.S. presence did not survive the decade after the end of the war for the liberation of Kuwait. While the Gulf Arabs acknowledged the need for U.S. protection and monitoring of the uneasy set of relationships between the GCC states and Iraq and Iran, those governments that were pro-Western or pro-American in orientation began to feel uneasy about life with only one superpower. They welcomed a U.S.-created and sustained coalition when Iraq invaded Kuwait for its ability to provide protection against real and potential aggressors and to help the Gulf return to peace and stability. But Gulf governments, in particular the Saudi ruling family, began to come under domestic criticism for hosting the U.S. military presence and for spending riyals on expensive military hardware while the government remained unable to defend the country. This criticism expanded by the late 1990s to include anti-American sentiment in the other Gulf states, including Kuwait. Moreover, with the exception of the UAE, the Gulf states were much more complacent about similar potential threats from Iran. Hopeful that President Mohammad Khatami's election presaged changes in Iran's Islamic militancy toward them, they have welcomed all signs of moderation in Iran and rejected any suggestion that Tehran supports terrorism or intends to threaten them once it has developed the technology for and tested new, more sophisticated long-range missiles that could carry biological or chemical warheads. Similarly, the GCC states have shrugged off dire predictions of the dangers of a nuclear-armed Iran.

Today, the security preference of most Gulf governments is to reestablish the kind of balance of power in the Gulf they once felt comfortable under—a balance maintained by friendly relations with a major regional power and backed up by a more distant U.S. presence. Except for Kuwait, Iraq's Gulf neighbors appear to believe that the war and sanctions have eroded Iraq's military capabilities to the point that they perceive little immediate threat. (Long accustomed to depending on foreign—usually Western—governments for their security needs, the Gulf states are weak on long-term strategic planning.) They are also moving cautiously in developing ties to Iran. Those ties, for now and the foreseeable future, will be limited to cooperation on trade, commerce, police matters, and sharing of intelligence on drugs and narcotics trafficking. They are not likely to conclude any significant security pact whose terms would include a demand for the withdrawal of U.S. military forces from the region. Gulf governments prefer to avoid antagonizing their larger and dangerous neighbors, but they also realize that American commitments to their security and a presence, however invisible they may pretend it is, allow them the freedom to negotiate with former enemy Iran and, at some point in the future, current enemy Iraq.

Domestic Determinants of GCC Security Policies

Contrary to the popular image, the Persian Gulf region has been remarkably stable over the past quarter century. Three major events have rocked the region: the Islamic revolution in Iran, the 8-year war between Iraq and Iran, and Iraq's invasion and occupation of Kuwait. Yet, with the exception of Iran, regional governments have remained stable and virtually unchanged. Saudi Arabia, Kuwait, Oman, Bahrain, Qatar, and the UAE are still ruled by the same families, although father-to-son successions have occurred in Bahrain, Qatar, and Dubai (part of the UAE). In Saudi Arabia, the running of government affairs has passed from an ailing King Fahd to his half-brother, Crown Prince Abdallah, while in Kuwait power is slipping from the hands of Amir Jabir al-Ahmad and his designated successor and cousin, Crown Prince Sa`d al-Abdullah (both of whom are in their late 70s and ill), to another aging family member, Foreign Minister Sabah al-Ahmad. Even Iran, the only country in the region to undergo a revolution in the last 20 years, has passed power to new leaders through elections.

Transfers of power within the GCC states have generally been orderly and preordained by elections or family, tribal and/or party consensus.

At the same time, as noted in the preceding chapter, the economies of the GCC states have remained stagnant, and stubborn demographic trends—rapidly increasing populations and lowered mortality rates—combined with growing unemployment and insufficient job creation seem poised to threaten stability. Population growth rates in Saudi Arabia and the smaller Gulf states are, at well over 3 percent per year, among the highest in the world, while the population of Iraq has risen from 19 million in 1990 to approximately 23 million in the year 2000, according to Iraqi statistics and despite war and sanctions. Overall populations are burgeoning even though fertility rates for women have been falling. Even if total population figures are somewhat exaggerated for domestic and regional political reasons, the populations of all the countries in the Gulf region at current rates of increase could double in 25 years. In 2002, 66 percent of the Muslim Middle East population was under 30, 50 percent under 20, and 40 percent under the age of 15.[4] As a result, an enormous demographic bulge in the younger age categories will continue to work its way through the school system and into the work force over the next decade. The immediate consequences of this demographic change are clear: greater demands on an unchanging social and economic infrastructure (for example, schools, roads, electricity, water, health care) and thus greater demands on the state. Lack of job creation—Iran has more than a million school graduates annually but can only generate approximately 300,000 new jobs—lack of housing, and lack of hope for a better future already plague Iran, where several cities have seen riots on these issues, and Iraq in particular.

Depressed oil prices have made it more difficult for the Gulf states' ability to provide the social services their populations expect. Saudi Arabia, for example, has experienced several years of budget deficits, and Riyadh is looking to increase user fees for goods and services, including electric rates, gasoline prices, and health care for expatriates. Most nationals work in government sector jobs; most private sectors jobs are held by expatriates, who are cheaper to hire and easier to fire. Approximately 75 percent of the estimated 8 million workers in Saudi Arabia are foreign workers. Privatizing state-owned service industries could mean more foreign workers, despite calls to Saudi-ize the work force and to increase prices but not efficiencies. New infrastructure investments will require large amounts of private capital, since even the Saudi state no longer has the resources to upgrade the power and water sectors, but wealthy natives tend to invest their money outside the region, in Western Europe or the United States, and the Saudi government has been unable to attract significant foreign investment.

Changes in education parallel the demographic boom. More Gulf students—especially in Saudi Arabia, the UAE, and Qatar—are being educated in government-funded schools in their home countries. Graduates no longer automatically look abroad for their university education and advanced degrees, meaning that fewer students in the rising generation will have a direct knowledge of or experience in the West or the United States. Higher literacy rates and university diplomas do not necessarily mean a better-educated or technologically prepared work force. Most students—perhaps as many as 80 percent—receive some amount of religious education from primary through university level, often to the detriment of the hard sciences and the liberal arts. Many Saudis, for example, will have graduated from the Islamic university system with degrees in Islamic law, sciences, or religious studies. These students may be swayed by a more conservative and religiously framed point of view, while others develop more nationalist political mindsets. They will not, however, be advocates of Western-style political institutions or practices or participate constructively in participatory government should political reforms occur. Above all, they will not be equipped to enter a 21st-century labor force demanding technical skills and experience. The disconnect between education and economy is especially pronounced among young women, who make up more than 50 percent of student bodies yet have no place in the economy because of local custom and religious restrictions.

The generation coming of age in this decade will not have experienced war or revolution. They did not fight in the Arab-Israeli or Gulf wars and have only seen the Palestinian side of the *intifada*, with its wanton violence, on television. Most have known only one ruler or, as in Bahrain and Qatar, a change of ruler but not of system. The rising generation in the oil-rich GCC states does not remember a time when there was poverty, before the exploitation of oil and the creation of a state-supported welfare system that guaranteed all citizens free health care, education, and a general sense of well being.

Domestic social and economic woes—such as drugs, support for extremist Islamist movements engaged in terrorism, and the increasing popularity of religiously defined political activist movements—are growing. Worries about what Iraq or Iran are contemplating or the need to counter

WMD proliferation are much less important security concerns than are these domestic troubles when added to demands for greater government accountability and modest (by Western standards) calls for political reform. Islamic extremists probably will not replace any Gulf governments, but their criticisms of the ruling families and attacks on government policies are shaping political and foreign policy agendas in the region, including Saudi Arabia and Kuwait.

External Drivers of GCC Security Policies

The greater the regional turmoil, the stronger is the longing of the GCC governments for a secure, stable, and recognizable balance of power. In 2003, the GCC states must decide how much support they can afford to give to the American war on terrorism and how much support they can afford to withhold from Saddam Husayn without rankling public opinion. They must calculate how to leverage the American need for their investment money and secure oil supplies at a stable price against seeming unrestrained U.S. support for Israel. They are prepared to live with a weakened Saddam (their perspective of his current position) or a suitable Sunni Arab successor and hopes of an increasingly moderate Iran, even if it does acquire WMD and the long-range missiles to deliver them. They are not happy with the thought of an unresolved and unresolvable Palestinian crisis, or with submitting to American demands for unlimited cooperation in a domestic hunt for supporters of al Qaeda and Osama bin Laden. The dilemma for the GCC states, therefore, is to balance a still necessary U.S. military presence against gradually improving relations with Tehran and, ultimately, Baghdad.

GCC Views of Iraq: Balancing Risk and Renewal

Probably the most difficult decision for the Gulf Arabs and Iran has been deciding how close to embrace Iraq without giving undue support to its quarrelsome leader. Saddam Husayn has outlasted two devastating wars, two major if disorganized rebellions, four U.S. Presidents, 12 years of sanctions, and the loss of much of his highly valued programs to build and acquire weapons of mass destruction. He has also survived U.S. efforts to declare him a pariah, isolate his government, and force compliance with UN Security Council resolutions aimed at eliminating his WMD and conventional weapons programs. He is using the Palestinian-Israeli violence to ensure his role as defender of the Palestinians, to portray himself as the only Arab and Muslim ruler to stand up to the United States and the only oil power willing to cut off oil to the United

States, and to patch up grievances between Iraq and Iran, Saudi Arabia, the other Arab states, and perhaps even Kuwait. In doing so, he has gained their backing to end sanctions.[5]

From the perspective of the Gulf Arabs, the options for dealing with Saddam are few and simple: sanction him, ignore him, accept him as the ultimate survivor, or pray someone will eliminate him. Sanctioning him and seeking to eliminate him as the ruler of Iraq are options that the United States is willing to pursue, but both pose domestic political difficulties for the GCC states. Ignoring Saddam or accepting him, while preferable to some in the Gulf, remain unacceptable choices for the United States. Whatever the option, Saddam Husayn and the regime he heads cannot be ignored, accepted, or eliminated without great risk, one that the GCC states see as primarily their own.

Sanctioning Saddam

The UN Security Council initially imposed sanctions on Iraq in the immediate aftermath of the invasion of Kuwait as a means of pressuring Saddam Husayn to withdraw without the need for force. The sanctions prohibited UN member states from importing Iraqi products, including oil, or exporting anything to Iraq other than food and medicine. The sanctions were kept in effect after the war in a slightly restructured form. Two broad categories of sanctions remained in effect after the Iraqi surrender. The first, economic sanctions, could be lifted when Iraq was found by the UN Security Council to be in compliance with the cease-fire resolution, particularly with the provisions calling for elimination of Iraq's biological, chemical, and nuclear weapons and long-range ballistic missiles. The second set of sanctions prohibits the sale of military hardware to Iraq and must be removed by a separate UN Security Council vote.

Sanctions worked in denying Saddam full sovereignty and unfettered use of Iraq's oil revenues, in weakening his military, and in denying him the ability to acquire easily components necessary to rebuild his conventional weapons systems or reconstitute wholesale WMD programs. Because of U.S. responses, moreover, Saddam has been unable to threaten his neighbors seriously, although there have been military feints and rhetorical warnings against Kuwait and other governments allowing the United States access to military facilities. The Gulf governments, however, hoped for much more. They expected that at some point Saddam would be forced to comply with the cease-fire terms in order to alleviate the suffering of the Iraqi people or, alternatively, that Iraqis would become so frustrated by hardship as well as by their political, economic, and diplomatic isolation that they would overthrow Saddam. But sanctions have not modified Saddam's behavior or changed his aggressive nature and the brutality of his regime. Nor have they made him willing to forgo possession of his weapons of mass destruction. Their success was due to the consensus of the international community that sanctions were the proper tactic to apply until Saddam complied with UN resolutions. That consensus has long been eroding.

The Gulf Arab states were among the first to abandon the international consensus on the open-ended maintenance of economic sanctions, in large measure because of public reaction to accounts of poor health conditions and malnutrition in Iraq. These concerns were not without a basis in the facts. While Iraq provides the only statistics available, which are therefore not independently verifiable, UNICEF reports that infant mortality has doubled since sanctions were imposed in 1990. UNICEF reports young children are chronically malnourished and that diarrhea is the major killer of the young.

U.S. efforts to lay the blame for this state of affairs on Saddam Husayn—to make the case that the international community cared more for the welfare of the Iraqi people than did their president—had little resonance in the Gulf. Saddam resisted accepting the first oil-for-food resolution (UNSCR 986) as yet another symbol of humiliation, but he was forced to accept it in 1996, 5 years after it was first proposed, almost certainly because he was unable to supply his loyal support base in the military and security services. This resolution allowed Iraq to sell $1.8 billion worth of oil every 6 months. By 1999, the amount of oil Iraq could sell had risen to $5.2 billion every 6 months and since then to virtually whatever it could sell.

This additional income should have allowed Saddam to provide much-needed goods for Iraqis suffering under sanctions. In the predominantly Kurdish north, where Iraqis are not in charge of food and humanitarian aid distribution, living conditions improved and the deaths of children under 5 years of age dropped from 80 per 1,000 live births from 1984 to 1989 to 72 per 1,000 between 1994 and 1999. Conditions did not necessarily improve in the areas under Saddam's control. In central and southern Iraq, where the regime is in control, the result of 12 years of sanctions has been the impoverishment of Iraq's traditional middle class of bureaucrats, technocrats, intellectuals, professionals, and civil servants, and higher mortality rates for the old, the weak, the children, and those otherwise undervalued or dispossessed by the regime, such as Shiah areas of southern Iraq that had engaged in the 1991 rebellion.

Infant mortality, according to Iraqi statistics (the only ones available), has doubled since sanctions were imposed, with the death rate for children under 5 rising from 56 per 1,000 live births from 1984 to 1989 to 131 per 1,000 between 1994 and 1999. Yet, while claiming Iraqis are starving because of sanctions, Baghdad has been caught trying to export baby food and medicine.

In short, Saddam has been able to divert attention and public anger in the Gulf away from his internal policies of punishing potential opponents by withholding access to food and medicine and hoarding imported goods for his supporters. Instead, he has successfully blamed the West—and specifically the United States and the United Kingdom—for the deaths of Iraqi children, for the increased incidence of malnutrition and disease, and for the impoverishment of the Iraqi middle class, leading Iraq's neighbors in the Arab world to conclude that sanctions are harming only the innocent people of Iraq and not the regime itself. Indeed, many in the Gulf argue that by crushing the middle class, whom they claim to see as a potential source of opposition, the sanctions have only strengthened the regime. Moreover, some note, the oil-for-food program has only magnified this problem by giving the regime monopoly control over the sale and distribution of all humanitarian goods entering the country.

As a result, although the Gulf governments agree with the United States that Iraq has not complied with UN Security Council resolutions on weapons inspections, they increasingly argue against what they see as sanctions without end and without incentive. Virtually all Arab and Muslim states inside and outside the Gulf hold this position. Arab public opinion and Islamist critics of Arab regimes sympathize with the Iraqi people. Arab governments, in increasing numbers, are seeking ways to join the public consensus without openly forgiving Saddam. Dissent to sanctions policy and sympathy for Iraq's people are growing even in Riyadh and Kuwait City, bringing with it the risk of criticism of the regimes for maintaining the embargo at the expense of Arab and Muslim self-interest. Since October 2000, many countries—including the UAE, Iran, and usually pro-Western Muslim states such as Turkey, Jordan, Tunisia, and Morocco—have flouted the embargo on civil air traffic to fly people and humanitarian goods directly into Baghdad.

Gulf Arabs see the pictures of Iraqis suffering under what are popularly perceived to be U.S.-imposed sanctions. They do not understand that eliminating sanctions will not mean immediate recovery for Iraq or its long-suffering people. Under the best of circumstances and with the highest oil prices, it will take years to rebuild Iraq. Iraq has and will long continue to have a desperate need for development assistance, water purification plants, sewage treatment facilities, and adequately staffed and supplied health care centers not controlled by the regime. The question is, what would be the effect on Gulf security of an Iraq liberated from intrusive controls? If recognizing Saddam meant more outside experts and observers in Iraq to work on project aid and more Iraqis permitted to leave Iraq, then it might have been worth it once. Now, it is almost certainly too late.

As seen from the GCC states, the object of sanctions and UN resolutions is to prevent Iraq from threatening their security, not least by ridding Iraq of its weapons of mass destruction. As much as regional rulers fear Saddam, for the states of the lower Persian Gulf he is not the issue and for the Saudis he is certainly part of the issue but not the whole issue. For Washington, however, Saddam *is* the issue. He is seen as the prime threat to regional security. U.S. policymakers assume his objectives and behavior are unlikely to change while he is in power and that only his removal will offer hope for change. In contrast, the GCC states have generally concluded that regime change from within is unlikely and, if it were to occur, would at best produce no shift in policy. At worst, they see it leading to instability, the disruption of the regional balance of power, and possibly the breakup of Iraq or its rule by an unstable democratic coalition or Iranian-influenced Shiah elements. They fear that any effort to change the regime in Baghdad will ultimately fail and that the United States will then leave its partners alone to face a vindictive, rearmed Saddam. They are for the most part, therefore, skittish about efforts to change the regime and argue instead that policy change could occur under Saddam. They say they are willing to deal with him, although with considerable reserve.

If Saddam is *not* to be removed from power, it is difficult to see what tactics are available to the Gulf governments to get him to behave. Will isolation or engagement work, punishment or incentives? Why should sanctions and pressure work now when Baghdad is gathering support, though neither worked earlier when Iraq stood alone? More tightly focused, or so-called smart, sanctions require the cooperation of countries shipping goods to Iraq as well as the support of Iraq's neighbors— and they have indicated their reluctance to support obtrusive inspections of goods entering and exiting Iraq. Like Russia and many European governments, most regional leaders argue that engagement and not isolation or punishment by military attack are the keys to defusing crises with Baghdad. They hold out hope that previous UN resolutions, which have been deliberately ambiguous in offering Baghdad temporary relief from economic sanctions if it complies with weapons inspections,[6] will permit a controlled opening—gradual sanctions relief, modest diplomatic engagement, opening cultural centers, and unfreezing assets—and a return to normalcy. But the hope that a solution can be found in a new, tougher inspections regime flies in the face of experience. Baghdad has no intention of complying with UNSC resolutions, especially on biological or chemical weapons programs—unless, perhaps, Saddam comes to the conclusion that the only choice he has is between disarmament and his own survival.

Unsanctioning Saddam

Without sanctions, what reason or incentive would Iraq have to abide by UN resolutions? The answer, quite simply, is none. Saddam effectively ended the UNSCOM monitoring and inspection regime by denying inspectors access to sites. He has continued his practices of denial and deception with the UN Monitoring, Verification, and Inspection Commission, which began inspections in December 2002. The independent activities of the UN and nongovernmental organizations in monitoring equitable food and humanitarian aid distribution would not be permitted. Efforts to get Iraq to acknowledge and return or account for missing Kuwaiti citizens and all property or to pay reparations would be scuttled. Saddam warned Iraqis in a speech in August 2000 not to "pay those to whom you are under no obligation more than their due." While this may be only a subtle hint at his unwillingness to continue to pay reparations, it came at the same time that the Kuwait Petroleum Company presented its claim for reparations. Payment into the compensation fund would become debt repayment to "friends." Money would be spent on domestic recovery, but few believe Saddam would delay military reconstruction for civilian redevelopment. Baghdad would even be likely to challenge the Kuwait-Iraq boundary settlement and the peacekeeping activities of the UN border observer mission.

In sum, the strategy of the Gulf states, focused solely on the immediate political costs of supporting either stiff containment or more assertive efforts at regime change, fails to take fully into account the longer-term strategic consequences of abandoning their support for sanctions that have impeded the development of Iraqi military capabilities. Do they really believe that Saddam would be a force for peace in the region or that he will be easier to deal with as his WMD capabilities grow? In 2002, Saddam offered support and cooperation to Arab consensus in support of the

Palestinians, sent emissaries to the GCC governments and the Arab League summit, and welcomed growing contacts and normalization of diplomatic relations with Iraq's neighbors and the region. Yet, only one year ago in a speech commemorating the end of the Iraq-Iran War, Saddam accused Turkey and the Gulf Arabs of "treachery and disgrace" for harboring the planes that kill the men, women, and children of Iraq. He criticized "those rulers and kings who have sold out their souls and appointed [the occupying foreigner] to rule over everything that is dear and precious in the values and wealth of their people."

Finally, there should be little doubt in the Gulf Arabs' minds that Saddam would pursue weapons of mass destruction. He did so while UNSCOM inspectors were operating in Iraq. It is possible to read Saddam's intentions in speeches made in the past 2 years. For example, on eliminating weapons systems, Saddam told officials of the Military Industrial Organization in June 2000 that he was willing to limit weapons on condition that Israel did so first. The evidence lies in what Baghdad has done in the nearly 4 years it went without inspections. Iraq test-fired a short-range, liquid-fueled ballistic missile—the al-Samoud (*resistance* in Arabic)—that could carry conventional explosives or the chemical or biological weapons that Iraq is still suspected of hiding.[7] American officials said the tests are evidence that Iraq is working to perfect its ballistic missile technology, which could be easily adapted to missiles with a longer range. The Iraqi declaration of its WMD programs and capabilities, submitted in compliance with UNSC 1441, was full of serious discrepancies, gaps, and omissions, indicating that Iraq continues its defiance of UNSC disarmament demands—a conclusion reinforced by Hans Blix, the head of UNMOVIC, and by information presented by U.S. Secretary of State Colin Powell in February to the UNSC.

Eliminating Saddam

Regional states have no appetite for continuing sanctions and other forms of intrusive containment of Iraq. However, their attitude toward U.S. military action to topple Saddam Husayn is more nuanced and ambiguous. To be sure, GCC states are reluctant publicly to support U.S. military operations to change the regime. Their lack of enthusiasm reflects a healthy fear of provoking Saddam anew by their opposition and domestic protests should they be seen to back American aggression against an Arab "hero" and the suffering people of Iraq. The GCC states would be more disposed to support a U.S. military operation if it were authorized by the UNSC and enjoyed broad international support, if it were quick, surgical, and decisive, or if the United States convinced them of its long-term commitment to building a non-threatening Iraq and offered a detailed and credible plan for how this goal would be accomplished. In any case, their willingness to throw in their lot with the United States on regime change will depend not only on how they judge American resolve, seriousness of purpose, and chances of success, but also on complex calculations about what their neighbors will do, what political and security price they will pay, whether they think the likely situation after regime change will be better or worse than what they are living with now, and how they could expect the United States to behave toward them after regime change under each of the various possible outcomes. Taking all these factors into account, it now appears as if the United States is likely to obtain the military cooperation it needs from Kuwait, Saudi Arabia, Qatar, and the other GCC states to mount an invasion of Iraq.

That said, Gulf Arab governments are reluctant to encourage actions in support of Iraqi opposition elements inside or outside Iraq. Once open to the possibility of acquiescing to U.S. requests to provide support to Iraqi dissidents from their territory, the Gulf Arabs are now much less willing to consider this option. Having viewed the mixed results of American efforts to work with the Iraqi National Congress (INC) and other anti-Saddam factions and aware of Baghdad's ability to penetrate many of the clandestine organizations, Gulf Arabs simply do not want to take the risk of provoking Saddam for an apparently feckless venture. Leadership rivalries and disagreements over tactics among the exiles simply reaffirm Gulf government suspicions about their potential effectiveness. Without proven credibility, there is little chance that the Gulf Arabs—let alone Jordan or Turkey—could be induced to take the risks implicit in allowing these groups to operate from their soil.

The Gulf Arabs are especially suspicious of two elements within the Iraqi opposition, whose presence is necessary to give the opposition credibility and military effectiveness: the Kurds of northern Iraq and the Iraqi Shiah factions based in Iran. The two major Kurdish factions (the Kurdish Democratic Party led by Masud Barzani and the Patriotic Union of Kurdistan led by Jalal Talabani) and the major Shiah opposition group, the Supreme Council for the Islamic Revolution in Iraq led by an Iraqi Arab cleric, Ayatollah Muhammad Baqr al-Hakim, are no longer part of the INC. They are the warfighters of the Iraqi opposition; without them operating against the regime in Iraq, there is no Iraqi Liberation Army.[8] Adding them to the mix raises the specter of the two least favorable outcomes envisioned by Gulf Arabs in an Iraq without Saddam: either a breakup of the country with the Kurds separating from Iraq or the ascent to power of the Shiah majority and the establishment of democratic pluralism in a new Iraq.

In sharp contrast to the United States, Iraq's Arab neighbors would prefer a successor who would be able to establish quickly and thoroughly his control over the country and its fractious ethnic, tribal, and religious elements without regard to democratic niceties. At least in the short term, the fears of Iraq's neighbors would be calmed because Saddam's successor would probably be a Sunni Arab. After all, Sunni Arabs, although only 17 percent of the population, have dominated Iraqi politics since the time of the Ottoman Empire. Moreover, political coalitions have never fared well in Iraq; the last coalition from the revolution of July 17, 1968, lasted less than 2 weeks. Even Iran would probably prefer as a short-term solution a known successor who could prevent the breakup of Iraq, the secession of the Kurds, civil war, or political chaos. In the longer term, Iran will expect to see Iraq move to a form of government similar in style (a republic), composition (pluralism and elections guaranteeing the Shiah and other elements their rightful place in governing Iraq), and ideology (Islamic). The Gulf Arabs, on the other hand, would be more than satisfied with a Sunni Arab strongman who merely renounced the expansionist ambitions that have characterized the present regime.

A coup by military or political factions that removed Saddam and left a prominent figure from his regime in power would almost certainly be welcomed by Iraq's neighbors and by European and Asian governments longing to deal with Baghdad again. Gulf Arabs would be relieved if that were palatable to U.S. policymakers, but American approval would not be necessary. The rush to approve a successor regime that was "Anyone But Saddam" could preempt a U.S. decision to deny or delay recognition in order to influence Baghdad's new government. If a coup removes Saddam and sons, Iraq's neighbors would hope that quick recognition of the new regime would enable it to hold the country together. The Gulf Arabs would have little interest in the form of government to be reconstructed in Iraq, so long as it were led by a strong Sunni Arab military figure with little interest in sharing power with the Shiahs or extending autonomy to the Kurds.

Given these regional preferences, if the United States is determined to effect more far-reaching regime change in Iraq, then it must be prepared to do some heavy lifting in the Gulf if it wishes to secure Gulf state support for its post-war settlement and reconstruction plans. It must also be prepared to answer some difficult questions:

- What is the objective? Is it just to eliminate Saddam and his immediate cohort, or is it to establish a radically different system of government and, if so, what kind?
- Is this system one that Gulf monarchs will find congenial or one that conforms to U.S. standards of democracy and human rights, regardless of the neighbors' preferences?
- What size occupation force will be needed, and how long will the United States need to remain in Iraq after Saddam is removed?
- How much disruption and instability is likely in the process of changing the regime, and how much will the United States tolerate?
- Perhaps most importantly, what is the risk to regional stability if and when Saddam is removed, and what is America prepared to do to ensure regional stability and Gulf regime security?

The United States needs to be ready with answers to Gulf regime concerns if one Sunni Arab replaces another Sunni Arab in Baghdad, or if a democratic coalition were installed that could lead to elections and, in theory, a Shiah majority in government. What is the United States prepared to do if, in the worst case, warlordism arises in Iraq, with factions and tribes and ethnic and sectarian violence creating chaos and disorder? All of these are reasonable concerns on the part of the Gulf regimes and ones that the United States must be prepared to address if it hopes to establish a viable multilateral approach to regime change. It is important, however, for the Gulf states to bear in mind that, notwithstanding their resources, Gulf state leverage over U.S. policies toward a post-Saddam government would be significantly reduced if the United States is successful in overthrowing the Ba´thists, and particularly if this result is achieved without the assistance of the Gulf states. Under these circumstances, for example, the United States would have far less incentive to give weight to Saudi preferences.

GCC Views of Iran: Hidden Risks and Opportunities

Shiah Islam, the religion of 90 percent of Iran's population, has a custom born of repression and life as a minority culture. The custom is called *taqiyah* and is sometimes defined as deception; it is a way of denying publicly to the dominant political culture (usually Sunni) what is practiced or acknowledged privately (Shi`ism).[9] In a sense, trying to divine Iranian official views on expanding ties to the once-despised Gulf Arab monarchs or to reestablishing relations with the United States and to calculate what gestures to make falls under a similar definition. What one sees in public discourse is not what one may hear in private conversation.

Gulf Arab leaders hope that Iran under President Khatami and the reformists will continue its uneven but determined pursuit of improving ties with the West and the United States. However, Khatami is now serving his second and final term, while the reformists must withstand continual battering from the conservatives. Following earlier and encouraging signs from the United States regarding cooperation on Afghanistan, Iran now feels rebuffed by charges that it is working against U.S. interests in Afghanistan and accusations that it supports terrorism through arms sales and financial assistance to Palestinian terrorists. The label of "axis of evil" had the unintended consequence of drawing Iran's disparate political factions closer together. Long criticized for its opposition to the peace process and support for Palestinian extremists, Tehran feels vindicated by the widespread regional support for the embattled Palestinians and against America.

Iranian Security Perceptions and GCC Defense Policy Choices

Three fundamental factors shape Iran's self-image: Iran as national identity and regional power, Islam as faith and ethical code, and Persia as source of history and future national prestige. Iran's foreign and security policy goals under the ayatollah or shah have remained the same: security of Iran's territorial and political integrity, recognition of regime legitimacy, and acknowledgment of the country's security concerns and historic regional leadership role. Iran's leaders see their country as encircled by real and potential enemies: Iraq, which used chemical weapons against Tehran in the 8-year war; the Gulf Arab states, which host the U.S. military presence and repress their Shiah communities; Pakistan, which is occasionally involved in hostile skirmishes with Iran on their mutual border and encouraged anti-Iranian activity in Afghanistan; and Central Asia, once under Russia's sway, now a source of economic opportunity, sectarian risk, and host to U.S. military forces. Above all, the United States and Israel are viewed as enemies, with Washington seen as keen to keep the Persian Gulf as its militarized zone, to place a pro-America regime in Baghdad and Kabul, and to militarize Central Asia.

Iran's leaders, whether moderate Persian nationalist or conservative Islamist, view the world with trepidation. Regardless of where they stand on the political spectrum, they likely share a common view of the threats to the security of the Iranian homeland and the measures necessary to protect Iran. Several factors shape this strategic and military thinking:

■ *The need for an enhanced capability to defend Iran, without any out-side help, against any threat of military aggression.* Tehran wants in-dependence and self-sufficiency in strategic and tactical terms. It believes it must build its own military industries, reconstitute a modern military force, and have minimal reliance on foreign sup-pliers. At the same time, Tehran is acquiring nuclear weapons to compensate for its military weakness and relative strategic isolation.

■ *The need to reassert Iran's traditional role of regional hegemon in the Gulf and beyond.* Iran's leaders believe it is Iran's natural right and destiny to dominate the region as well as lead the world's Muslims. Moreover, they believe Iran has a direct interest in all matters re-gional and Islamic, including in the Gulf and the Levant. Despite a prohibition by the late Ayatollah Khomeini against relations with the Saudis, the Iranian government values its new and expanding ties to Saudi Arabia and the other Gulf Arab regimes to reduce ten-sions in the Gulf and gain political and economic support. Even the UAE maintains links to Iran, despite their seeming intractable dis-pute over ownership of three small islands in the Gulf, the Greater and Lesser Tunbs and Abu Musa. The Gulf regimes, moreover, are skeptical that they can do anything to prevent Iran from acquiring nuclear weapons capability or longer-range ballistic missiles and look to the United States to provide an effective deterrent to Iranian WMD threats.[10]

The Containment Option

Although the Gulf states appreciate the counterweight the United States provides to Iran, they have long deplored what they see as the self-defeating nature of key elements of the U.S. policy of containing Iran, a pol-icy that relies primarily on isolation, pressure, and punishment (for exam-ple, sanctions) to end Iranian support for international terrorism, opposition to the Middle East peace process, and efforts to acquire weapons of mass destruction. The sanctions include a trade embargo and punish-ment of those who provide investment and development assistance to Iran.

Scholars and analysts disagree on the impact of sanctions, but one thing is clear: sanctions, including the arms embargo and efforts to block foreign loans to and investment in Iran, have delayed but not denied Iran the ability to procure the expertise, technology, and material for noncon-ventional weapons. Spending on conventional military capabilities did not reach the levels U.S. Government experts estimated they would reach in the early 1990s. At the same time, demands for domestic spending on subsidies, job creation, and economic infrastructure in years of low oil prices did not preclude spending on acquisition of NBC technology. In fact, low oil prices and domestic economic woes probably did more damage to Iran's economy than sanctions. U.S. sanctions policy, however, has fed Gulf Arab unease with American policies that it believes ignore their interests. Like Europe, Gulf governments prefer a policy of engagement and critical dialogue with Iran and not containment and isolation. Gulf Arabs would prefer that the United States drop economic sanctions on Iran and encourage, instead, foreign investment in Iran's domestic and economic infrastructure.

Is Transparency Protection for the GCC?

Iranian leaders generally assume that the United States maintains a large military force in the Gulf to monitor Iran, not Iraq. They also assume that the United States is intent on militarizing Central Asia and installing pro-American governments in Kabul and Baghdad. Iran has indicated to the GCC states its preference that U.S. military forces be sent home and has offered to spread its protective wing over their Gulf state neighbors.

The GCC response, for the most part, has been transparency. Until the events of September 11, Gulf rulers talked about a lower profile for U.S. forces in the region, especially Saudi Arabia, and virtually all publicly disapproved use of their territory for offensive military operations against Iraq. Being risk averse, however, it is unlikely that the GCC would bend to requests from Tehran or Baghdad to lower or eliminate the presence of or their commitments to U.S. military forces and force protection. Instead, they hope that Iran's quest for friends in the Gulf, their own nonconfrontational diplomacy, plus transparency in military relationships and operations will allay Tehran's concerns and stave off an angry Baghdad. To prevent Iran from misinterpreting GCC and U.S. intentions and activities, they will encourage the United States to expand confidence building measures—such as help in demining, an incidents-at-sea agreement, and joint rescue exercises—and eventually support Iran's gradual inclusion in regional security discussions. This would not amount to a security pact or Iran's membership in the GCC or some other NATO-style arrangement. But it could mean a new channel where tensions could be reduced without the risk of military confrontation. This could include discussions with Tehran on Iraq's future after Saddam.

At the same time, the GCC countries will need to consider what measures they should take in the event a nuclear-armed Iran assumes a more menacing posture or a rearmed Iraq poses a threat to their security. Saudi Arabia and its partners in the GCC could choose to do nothing, join someone's nuclear umbrella, or acquire their own nuclear deterrents. The GCC states are consumers of security, vulnerable to attack from larger, more powerful neighbors if provoked. So far, they have chosen, for the most part, to rely on external alliances and arms to protect their security. The memory of Iraq's invasion of Kuwait should be sufficient reminder that threatening neighbors need to be counterbalanced, but memories fade fast, and there is an overwhelming desire on the part of most Arabs in the region to return to the policies of a simpler, distant era—before Baghdad's invasion of Kuwait. Conversely, a strategy of denial may not offer security. Two alternatives present themselves:

- *The GCC could ask the United States for expanded security guarantees and a smaller military presence.* In the face of a nuclear-armed Iran, or a rearmed Iraq, the Gulf Arabs are likely to seek expanded American guarantees of enhanced protection and promises to defend them if a confrontation is imminent. They are not likely, however, to support a U.S. policy of preemptive strikes to lessen their Iran problem. Like the Europeans, they instinctively shrink from the use of armed force to settle political problems. They will not join Iran in a security arrangement that would preclude an American presence in the Gulf, reflecting in part their understanding that the U.S. military presence increases their room to maneuver with Tehran and Baghdad. At the same time, most Gulf regimes fear popular protest over an American presence and dependence on it for protection that their governments should be able to provide.

- *The Gulf governments could seek new or additional U.S. military aid.* This carries risks. Israel is certain to oppose any Gulf Arab requests for U.S. weapons upgrades or new fighter aircraft, believing—incorrectly—that any new systems would be targeted on Israel and/or turned over to the Palestinians or Syrians for use against Israel. Force protection is an obvious concern, especially given the attack on the USS *Cole* in Aden, repeated threats from adherents of al Qaeda to strike again at U.S. forces and interests, and the impression that Saudi Arabia is less interested in protecting American forces than in restricting their presence and operations. The Gulf governments also could choose to acquire their own missile defense system. However, they are not seized with the urgency of the Iraqi or Iranian WMD threat and are likely to balk over the costs of deploying effective missile defenses. As discussed in chapter five, another possible but by no means assured outcome, given the negative domestic political implications, is some combination of Gulf state approval for the United States to deploy and operate its own missile defense systems on their territory and their acquisition of more capable units as they are fielded.

The Preferred GCC Option: U.S. Engagement of Iran

From the perspective of the GCC states, the most effective course for U.S. policy would be to continue to seek dialogue with Iran. American sanctions policy has inhibited some countries and companies from developing commercial and financial ties to Iran, but U.S. ability to dictate the terms of other governments' engagement with Iran is diminishing rapidly. In their view, engagement with Iran would seem more productive than trying to sustain the current containment policy. In this context, the Gulf Arab states would like to see the United States:

- stop vilifying Iran as a "rogue" state. Recognizing Iran's security perception and giving them a voice in a regional forum not only would allow Iran the political, economic, and strategic interaction it seeks but also would set the agenda and terms of engagement on the basis of Iran's behavior before it tries to make demands based on its nuclear status.
- work on topics of shared concern. The GCC, the United States, and Iran view Afghanistan, Iraq, and drug trafficking as serious threats to the security and stability of the Middle East and Central Asia.
- end the sanctions that preclude economic investment in Iran. Acquiescence to a pipeline project to carry Central Asian gas and oil would be an important signal of American awareness of Iran's economic needs, though it is problematic whether the Gulf states, who would see this development as competition, would support such an initiative. It could also defuse potential Iranian dependence on Chinese investment in the energy sector of its economy.

Conclusion

An American military presence in the Gulf will be required for some time; hence, the desire of the Gulf states to reduce the U.S. military footprint and the vulnerability of forward deployed forces needs to be balanced against the political and deterrent value of a visible U.S. military presence in the Gulf. If friends and enemies no longer see U.S. forces and operations, they may conclude that the Gulf governments are once again vulnerable to intimidation or outright threat and that America is less likely to defend its interests and honor its security commitments in the region. In approaching decisions on American future forward presence posture for the Gulf, several political realities need to be taken into account:

- Iraq and Iran are not universally perceived by the GCC states as major and imminent threats to regional security, and most believe the United States needs to shape strategies to engage Iraq and Iran positively. Kuwait, which does see Iraq as a serious threat, is an obvious exception, and many Saudis continue to mistrust and fear the Iraqi regime. But for the states of the lower Gulf (the UAE, Qatar, Bahrain, and Oman), Iran and in some cases disputes with each other loom much larger in their threat perceptions.

- The violence of the Israeli-Palestinian conflict, the intractability of Yasser Arafat and Ariel Sharon, and U.S. reluctance to take the lead in finding a solution are shaping GCC public attitudes and have damaged American influence in the region to a significant degree.

- President George W. Bush's description of Iran and Iraq as part of an "axis of evil" has had unintended and deleterious consequences for U.S. policy goals in the region.

- Support for sanctions against Iraq and pariah status for Saddam Husayn is evaporating.

- Political change in Iran may come smoothly or violently, but it will not alter a defense strategy based on a determination to acquire a nuclear capability, which has a geopolitical logic (Iraq on one side, a nuclear subcontinent on the other) that is hard to ignore. However, regime change in Iran could alter Iranian positions on a range of foreign policy issues, including on the Arab-Israeli issue and on questions of "political Islam" more generally.

Notes

[1] Saudi Arabia, Kuwait, Bahrain, Qatar, the United Arab Emirates, and Oman are the six full members of the Gulf Cooperation Council. In 2001, they extended a special status to Yemen.

[2] The United States first entered the Gulf with a small naval presence—the U.S. 5th Fleet—in 1948 in Bahrain; U.S. policy encouraged a balance of power that allowed the Shah to dominate the region. (The U.S. Air Force also was at Dhahran from the 1940s to the early 1960s.)

[3] The Rapid Deployment Joint Task Force became the U.S. Central Command in 1983; its mission was to "deter the Soviets and their surrogates from further expansion and, if necessary, defend against it."

[4] Alan Richards, "Global Economics: Gunning for the Root of 'Evil,'" *San Francisco Chronicle*, April 14, 2002.

[5] At the Arab League summit held in Beirut in March 2002, Saudi Crown Prince Abdallah extended the kiss of peace to Izzat Ibrahim, a deputy prime minister of Iraq and one of Saddam's closest and oldest supporters. Iraq also signed a memorandum with Kuwait in which Iraq recognized the territorial integrity and independence of the country it called its former 19th province following the 1990 invasion and occupation.

[6] The resolutions in theory combine a newly designed UN weapons inspection team—called UNMOVIC, or the UN Monitoring, Verification, and Inspection Commission—with the freedom of action (full, unfettered access to sites) accorded UNSCOM and a grace period for a compliant Iraq.

[7] The range of the missile was less than 150 kilometers (95 miles) and not in violation of UN Security Council resolutions that ban missiles with a range greater than 150 kilometers.

[8] The Kurdish factions, SCIRI, and a number of senior military and government defectors belonging to the Iraqi National Accord and other factions formed a new grouping in London in 2002. Described as the "gang of 4," it brings together prominent military and intelligence officers who served Saddam but who refuse to make common cause with the INC.

[9] As a religious concept, *taqiyah* allows a Shiah Muslim to dissimulate to save his life, but the concept also feeds into a broader cultural pattern of 2,000 years of court politics, where one conceals true motives to preserve ones options.

[10] Iran's newest missile—the Shahab-3—has a range of 1,200 kilometers, putting targets in Turkey, Israel, Iraq, and the Persian Gulf within its reach. See Kori N. Schake and Judith S. Yaphe, *The Strategic Implications of a Nuclear-Armed Iran* (Washington, DC: National Defense University Press, 2001).

Chapter Four

The Regional Military Balance

Kenneth M. Pollack

T he preceding discussion has made clear that the security environment in the Persian Gulf is likely to remain precarious and uncertain for the foreseeable future, with or without regime change in
Iraq or Iran. Both countries have aspirations for regional dominance and
view the U.S. military presence in the region, as well as America's security
relationships with the Gulf countries, as a threat to these ambitions.
Whether Iraq or Iran is tempted to challenge the geopolitical status quo
militarily will depend largely on the evolution of the regional military balance and their perceptions of the credibility of the U.S. military deterrent.

The new defense strategy adopted by the 2001 *Quadrennial Defense
Review Report* calls for a new framework for determining U.S. overseas
presence and reinforcement plans in all major theaters. The manner in
which this framework is applied to the Persian Gulf will be influenced
heavily by the evolving military balance among allies and adversaries there
and by the resulting need to apply American military power in ways that
deal with the new security challenges ahead. This chapter examines likely
developments in the regional force balance and the trends that will shape
the military capabilities of key regional actors.[1]

Iraq

Even if Saddam Husayn remains in power, the threat from Iraq to
the Gulf states is likely to remain limited for the foreseeable future. Under
almost any circumstances, Iraq will retain some limited offensive capability against the Gulf Cooperation Council (GCC) states and other weak
neighbors (Jordan and, to a lesser extent, Iran). However, the extent of
this threat depends heavily on the extent to which United Nations (UN)
sanctions remain on Iraq and are enforced by the international community. Under most scenarios, the Iraqi ability to defeat U.S. forces will be

nonexistent, especially given expected improvements in American capabilities over the next 10 years.

On the eve of the Persian Gulf War a decade ago, Iraq had one of the largest and best-armed military establishments in the world. With 55 divisions and over 600 combat aircraft, it was far stronger than Kuwait and Saudi Arabia and had ample forces for conducting a sweeping offensive against them. Ten years later, the Iraqi military still has not recovered from the devastation of the Gulf War. In terms of manpower, combat formations, and equipment holdings (shown in table 4–1 below), Iraq's military today is about 40 to 50 percent of its pre-Operation *Desert Storm* size. Qualitatively, it is in even worse shape. Moreover, with its economy a shambles, a gross domestic product (GDP) of only $16 billion, and annual defense spending of roughly $2 billion (compared to $14 billion in 1990), Iraq faces enormous financial difficulties in rectifying serious shortfalls in manning, training, exercises, logistics support, supplies, and war reserve stocks.

Iraq's weaponry was mostly a generation out of date before the Gulf War, and today it is approaching block obsolescence. For example, roughly one-third of its 2,200 tanks are T–72s, and the rest are mostly antiquated T–55s and T–62s. Of its 2,100 artillery tubes, only 150 are self-propelled and the remainder towed. Most of the 316 combat aircraft in its inventory are Soviet-built models at least 15 to 20 years old that lack modern sensors, munitions, and command, control, communications, computers, intelligence, surveillance, and reconnaissance support. Iraq's navy operates only

Table 4–1. **Iraqi Military Forces, 1990–2001**

Category	1990	2001
Military personnel	1,100,000	424,000
Tanks	5,700	2,200
Other armored fighting vehicles	8,000	3,500
Artillery pieces	3,100	2,050
Combat aircraft	650	316 (approximately 100–150 operational)
Division equivalents	55	23
Defense budget (in billions of dollars)	13.0	1.4
Naval combatants	43	6

Source: International Institute for Strategic Studies, *The Military Balance, 1989–1990* and *The Military Balance, 2000–2001* (Oxford: Oxford University Press, 1989, 2000), and author's estimates.

a handful of patrol boats and mine warfare ships that are incapable of asserting control over the waters of the northern Persian Gulf.

Iraqi forces have also suffered a serious decline in readiness over the past decade. Most of Iraq's regular army divisions are reported as badly deficient in manpower and training, and much of their equipment lacks spare parts. Probably no more than one-half to one-third of Iraq's combat aircraft are serviceable. In addition, Saddam tightened his control over the armed forces in the last 10 years by establishing new command and control procedures that distort the chain of command, reintroducing "political commissars" (in the form of Special Security Organization personnel attached to all major field formations), and replacing many professional officers with his own loyalists. Training standards are still well below pre-Gulf War levels. Brigade-level exercises are sporadic and divisional exercises extremely rare. Many units lack the funds, equipment, and supplies to undertake rigorous training, and the pre-Gulf War training cycle has been reduced to account for these postwar realities. Because of the higher cost and greater demands of air operations, the Iraqi Air Force suffers from these problems to an even greater extent than the Iraqi ground forces. For example, Iraq's veteran combat pilots fly about 100 hours annually, while junior pilots fly 20 hours (compared to a U.S. training rate of 220 hours annually). Additionally, Operation *Southern Watch* has seriously degraded the capabilities and readiness of Iraq's air defense system.

Probably the most significant difference between the pre-Gulf War Iraqi armed forces and those of today is the precipitous decline of Iraqi logistics as a result of 10 years of sanctions. Before the Gulf War, the Iraqi military was able to move large armored forces great distances quickly and supply them over considerable stretches of territory and time. This ability was one of their strengths. However, sanctions have destroyed Iraq's lift and sustainment capacity. As an example, before the invasion of Kuwait, the Iraqis moved the entire Republican Guard (8 divisions, 120,000 men, 1,500 armored vehicles) an average of 600 kilometers to the Kuwaiti border in less than 2 weeks. By contrast, in the fall of 2000, the Iraqis found it impossible to move 5 divisions (with approximately 50,000 men and 500–600 armored vehicles) roughly 300 kilometers to the Syrian border. After 6 weeks of traffic jams and breakdowns, they simply gave up and sent the units back to their garrisons.

Maintenance in Iraqi field units is even worse than normal (and during the Iran-Iraq War, 50 percent operational readiness rates were common) because UN sanctions have choked off Iraq's access to spare parts, some lubricants, and many consumables. If Iraqi forces attempted an invasion of Saudi Arabia today, it is likely that maintenance problems would bring the drive to a halt far short of Dhahran even without U.S. intervention, with a long line of broken-down Iraqi armored vehicles stretching all the way back to al-Basrah. However, Iraq does not (and never did) have to drive to Dhahran to have a very serious impact on American interests. Absent U.S. military intervention, Iraq could successfully invade Kuwait, which would likely bring about undesirable changes in Saudi policies on a number of fronts.

Finally, Iraq has lost much of the expertise it gained during the Iran-Iraq War, which was one of its most important pre-Gulf War military assets. During the Iran-Iraq War, Saddam had allowed an extensive de-politicization of the Iraqi military. He permitted considerable numbers of competent Iraqi officers to move into command positions and allowed the development of a more professional military ethos. In particular, the Iraqi General Staff was manned by a highly competent group of professional officers who planned and directed the 5 Iraqi offensives in 1988 that succeeded in destroying Iran's ground forces and winning the war for Baghdad. Many of those officers are gone—either killed, retired, or purged when Saddam repoliticized the military after the Gulf War and the 1991 rebellions. Likewise, many of the troops and junior officers who fought the battles of the Iran-Iraq War have retired from active service. As a result, the Iraqi armed forces are no longer as experienced as they once were, far fewer of its men have ever been in combat, and far fewer of its officers would know how to conduct the meticulous, set-piece offensives that Iraq used to defeat Iran and overrun Kuwait.

Iraq's farcical declaration to the United Nations notwithstanding, there is little doubt that Iraq has been able to retain at least some limited weapons of mass destruction (WMD) capability, which likely includes some chemical warfare (CW) munitions, several dozen Scud-type ballistic missiles, and possibly some weaponized biological warfare (BW) agent. In addition, the al-Samoud and other short-range ballistic missiles that Iraq is developing, supposedly within the terms of the UN Security Council (UNSC)-mandated cease-fire, are unequivocally intended to give Iraq a head start on developing medium- and intermediate-range missiles as soon as the sanctions are lifted. Indeed, Hans Blix has declared that the al-Samoud range already exceeds the UN-imposed ceiling of 150 kilometers. For the most part, these residual weapons are intended as an ultimate deterrent for the regime and as the seeds for a full-blown Iraqi WMD program once sanctions are lifted. Western intelligence agencies seem to have reached a consensus that Iraq has resumed its efforts to build a nuclear weapon and has all of the equipment and know-how to do so; the only question is how long it will take Iraq to acquire sufficient fissile material. If Iraq is able to acquire weapons-grade fissile material on the black market, it might be able to build a nuclear weapon within 2 years. However, if Iraq is forced to enrich the material itself, as seems more likely, the process probably will require 4 to 6 years.

Given all of Iraq's current military deficiencies, if the United States were to mount a full-scale invasion to enforce the UN Security Council resolutions in the near term, the Iraqi armed forces would have tremendous difficulty coping with U.S. military operations. Assuming that the United States employed both large air and ground forces (400+ combat aircraft and 4 or more combat divisions), it is hard to imagine a scenario in which the Iraqi armed forces would be likely to defeat U.S. forces or prevent them from overrunning the country. The best that Iraqi forces might hope for would be to inflict enough casualties on U.S. forces and threaten other U.S. vital interests to such an extent that Washington would make the political decision to call off the invasion. This too would be difficult, but a far more realistic strategy than attempting to defeat U.S. forces outright.

In the event of a U.S. invasion of Iraq, Iraq's ability to inflict heavy casualties on U.S. forces would depend on a wide range of factors. Probably the most important of these variables, however, include how hard Iraqi soldiers would fight, to what extent they would be able to employ WMD against U.S. forces, and to what extent they could mount an effective defense of Iraq's cities—and force the U.S. military to engage in urban combat. On none of these counts should Baghdad be confident of the outcome. Nevertheless, it would also be unwise for U.S. decisionmakers to assume that Saddam Husayn would reach the same conclusions; Saddam is famous for making fantastic miscalculations, and, in snubbing the UN with a blatantly farcical WMD declaration in December 2002, Saddam appears to be strangely confident in his ability to prevail against the United States.

Although certainly possible, it would be very difficult for Iraq to mount a defense that inflicted severe (10,000 or more) casualties on U.S. forces in the course of a U.S.-led invasion. The best evidence available indicates that most Iraqi soldiers would offer little more than token resistance, and many would likely surrender or desert immediately if faced with a U.S.

offensive. Indeed, it is possible that the Iraqi armed forces would collapse altogether. While not likely, this scenario appears more probable than the alternative extreme of every Iraqi soldier fighting very hard. Thus, in the most likely scenario, Iraq's regular armed forces would offer only desultory resistance and only Saddam's Republican Guards, Special Republican Guards, and a number of other security personnel probably would be willing to fight to the death for the regime based on their behavior during the Gulf War and the *intifada* that followed. This could amount to roughly 100,000 to 150,000 men willing to fight hard for the Saddam regime.

A force of that size—armed, trained, and led as poorly as the Iraqi armed forces are—would have to rely on tactical use of WMD and the ability to mount effective urban combat operations to inflict heavy casualties on a large U.S. invasion force. This too would be difficult for Iraq. U.S. forces are quite well protected against tactical CBW use, certainly far better protected than the Iraqis themselves. In addition, the speed and dislocation of a U.S. offensive would likely make it hard for the Iraqis with their poor surveillance and targeting capabilities to locate and strike U.S. forces effectively. Moreover, American air forces (both fixed and rotary wing) would likely operate forward of U.S. ground forces, aggressively striking any concentrations of Iraqi artillery, multiple rocket launchers, decontamination units, and other assets required for Iraqi WMD use. American air defenses, both offensive and defensive, would also make it extremely difficult for Iraqi aircraft to strike U.S. ground forces with WMD. This suggests that Iraq may be able to employ WMD in a limited, desultory fashion that could inflict scores or even hundreds of casualties but would be unlikely to cause decisive losses.

Iraqi forces could no doubt hole up in at least several Iraqi cities but would find it difficult to mount cohesive urban defense operations that could greatly hinder or defeat a U.S. invasion force. First, a large enough American force could mask and bypass most Iraqi cities. Second, a U.S. offensive would likely move much faster than the Iraqi armed forces could handle, making it hard for them to improvise coherent defensive schemes. Third, given the limited number of troops that appear likely to remain loyal to Saddam, it would be difficult for the regime to mount effective defenses of more than a handful of cities—a division or a few brigades in a city of several hundred thousand people can cause casualties to a strong attacking force but cannot mount a coherent defense, especially against the modern urban assault tactics that American forces are likely to employ. The one exception is Baghdad where, if Saddam concentrated both the Special

Republican Guard and the Republican Guard in the city in pre-prepared defensive positions, he might present a formidable obstacle to U.S. forces. However, even there, the United States will have counters available—such as moving so quickly as to be on top of Baghdad before the Iraqi defenders are set and attacking the city in concentric fashion by taking down key movement corridors and dominant nodes, liberating the Shiah sectors whose denizens are likely to aid U.S. forces against Saddam and isolating and clearing sectors of the city to compromise its overall defenses.

In short, Iraq's ability to defeat a near-term U.S. invasion by inflicting enough casualties to convince Washington to call off the operation would be very limited. It is not impossible that if the Iraqis fight much harder than the available evidence suggests, they are able to use their WMD effectively and mount cohesive defenses of Iraq's cities—and if they can take advantage of American mistakes—they might be able to inflict as many as 10,000 casualties on U.S. forces. However, it is far more likely that an American invasion would succeed rapidly (in a matter of weeks) with most Iraqi forces surrendering or being overpowered while inflicting only light (500–1,000 combat deaths) casualties on U.S. forces.

If Saddam remains in power and the current panoply of sanctions remains in place, this assessment of Iraqi military strength is likely to remain relatively constant. Iraq will have to work hard simply to prevent a further decline. Unquestionably, Iraq has been able to smuggle in some spare parts and combat consumables even under the current sanctions regime. But just as clearly, this has not been a significant amount and certainly not enough to compensate for the continued erosion of Iraq's training, leadership, combat experience, and logistical capabilities along with the growing obsolescence of its equipment.

However, it seems unlikely that the sanctions regime will remain unchanged for long if Saddam is allowed to remain in power. The questions, to some extent, are how much it will change, and what difference it would make in Iraq's combat capabilities and the regional force balance. For instance, if the economic sanctions on Baghdad were suspended or lifted but the military embargo remained in place (the most likely near-term alternative to removing Saddam's regime), Iraq probably would be able to make a partial recovery of its pre-*Desert Storm* military strength. In particular, in this scenario, Baghdad would have unimpeded access to trucks, cars, tires, asphalt, rolling stock, locomotives, track, telecommunications gear, construction equipment, and all of the other supplies necessary to make railroads and wheeled vehicles work. This access would be a huge boon to Iraq's crippled logistics. Within as little as 3 to 5 years, Iraq might be able to recover its former logistical capabilities. In addition, the sense that Iraq's international isolation was ending would almost certainly improve Iraqi morale, as would the reviving of the Iraqi economy, which might make life easier for the families of soldiers and probably mean that the regime would have greater resources to reward loyal officers.

In addition, Iraqi WMD programs will benefit somewhat from a suspension of the economic sanctions. WMD programs require much smaller amounts of resources and equipment than conventional forces. Although some equipment is so specialized that it can have only one possible use, much of the equipment Iraq needs for its WMD programs falls into the dual-use category, which Baghdad may get access to if the economic sanctions are suspended. Moreover, the vast increase in trade moving in and out of Iraq under these circumstances will make smuggling much easier, and WMD items will undoubtedly get in no matter the degree of international vigilance. Because of the priority Baghdad is likely to attach to WMD items, and because comparatively few items are needed for these programs, smuggling could make a significant difference to Iraq's clandestine WMD programs.

Until the economic embargo is lifted, however, Iraq's overall military recovery will remain limited. Unchaining Iraq's civilian economy will expand the opportunities for smuggling, but as long as the military sanctions remain in place and enforced, Iraq will be unable to purchase the vast amounts of weapons, equipment, spare parts, ammunition, and other combat consumables it desperately needs. Rebuilding Iraq's conventional forces will be a monumental task, and the quantity and quality of goods Baghdad will be able to smuggle in will hardly make a dent in its needs.

As long as some form of sanctions remain on Iraq, Baghdad's ability to *use* any of its weapons of mass destruction for coercive purposes will be constrained. Any Iraqi threats or use of these weapons would destroy Baghdad's carefully constructed lie that it has no weapons of mass destruction and that it has learned its lesson about WMD use. Saddam's prospects for ending Iraq's diplomatic isolation and having the remaining sanctions lifted would evaporate, and Saddam would have to fear that the international community would essentially give the United States carte blanche to "solve the problem" of Iraq however it saw fit. This equation would change, however, if meaningful sanctions were no longer in place, or if Iraq no longer had any incentives to continue concealing violations of UNSC resolutions.

It is for this reason that Baghdad has viewed—and probably will continue to view—its existing WMD arsenal as a deterrent of last resort rather than another tool in its foreign policy kit for as long as military sanctions remain in place. However, under circumstances in which the survival of the regime is at stake, Iraqi threats to use, or actual use of, chemical and biological weapons to deny U.S. forces access to the region pose a potentially significant military problem. This would be the case, for example, if Saddam threatened to attack Saudi Arabia, Bahrain, or any of the other GCC states if they allowed U.S. reinforcements to enter their country. To give credibility to these threats, Iraq could conduct a limited BW strike on key reception facilities in Saudi Arabia or elsewhere in the Gulf if it believed that it was in dire straits. Given American dependence on host nation support at aerial ports of debarkation and seaports of debarkation, such attacks could slow the rate at which the United States deploys forces to the region, making forward defense at the Kuwaiti-Iraqi border problematic. Moreover, even if Iraq does not acquire long-range missiles with WMD warheads, it might increase the size and accuracy of its Scud force and possibly acquire conventionally armed cruise missiles. As highlighted in the following chapter, such missiles, along with naval mines and other weapons, could pose a growing antiaccess/area denial threat to U.S. forces and local infrastructure, thereby impeding the ability to deploy swiftly to the Gulf in time to defeat a surprise Iraqi attack.

The one aspect of Iraq's WMD programs that could radically alter the regional balance and Iraqi behavior would be Baghdad's acquisition of nuclear weapons. The best available evidence regarding Saddam Husayn's thinking about nuclear weapons is that he believes that they will fundamentally alter the balance of power between Iraq and the world, including specifically the United States. He apparently believes that once Iraq possesses nuclear weapons, short of a direct attack on the U.S. homeland, Washington would not dare to oppose virtually any Iraqi action in the region—including new aggression or blackmail against Iraq's neighbors. He has long believed that possession of nuclear weapons was a critical element of realizing his plan to make Iraq into a new superpower. Saddam has long coveted nuclear weapons because (in the words of his half-brother and then chief of intelligence) "we want a strong hand in order to redraw the map of the Middle East." Thus, Iraq's acquisition of nuclear weapons would greatly increase the risk of war in the Gulf region because Saddam believes that they would effectively remove the United

States as an obstacle to his regional ambitions and negate the massive dis-
parity in conventional forces between Iraq and America.

Ultimately, it is unlikely that, even if all sanctions on Iraq are removed, the Iraqi armed forces will be able to do more than regain their
pre-Gulf War size and strength over the next 10 years—a capability that
would be no match for decisive U.S. military intervention. Were all sanctions on Iraq lifted or allowed to erode such that Iraq could import military equipment again, it will likely require 5 to 10 years just for Iraq to
make up its losses from the Gulf War and since. In addition to buying huge
amounts of new equipment—thousands of new tanks, armored personnel
carriers, artillery pieces, and surface-to-air missiles (SAMs); hundreds of
new combat aircraft; tens of thousands of support vehicles and crew-
served weapons; and hundreds of thousands of small arms—Iraq would
also have to expand its military personnel by as much as one-quarter- to
one-half-million men. It will take many years just to fill out such a force
structure, train the men, and allow them to assimilate their new weapons.

Regaining its pre-Gulf War military strength would make Iraq far
more powerful than it is today but would hardly make it a military heavy-
weight compared to the United States fighting alongside its Gulf partners.
As *Desert Storm* made clear, even the Iraqi military of 1990 was little more
than a third-rate force compared to American military forces. The most
important reason for this is the longstanding military ineffectiveness of
Iraqi forces, which remains to this day and which Baghdad has made little
progress in overcoming. Since 1948, Iraq's military effectiveness has been
crippled by passive and unimaginative tactical leadership, poor combined
arms operations, miserable air operations, severely distorted information
flows, an inability to take full advantage of sophisticated weaponry, poor
maintenance, and badly outdated tactics. Iraq has not made any progress
in solving these much deeper problems, which would be very debilitating
if it were fighting U.S. forces—although considerably less so if it were
matched up against the Gulf Arabs or Iran. Consequently, even if Iraq were
to rebuild its forces quantitatively to their pre-Gulf War size and even if
they did so with more modern weapons, its military capability would remain far more modest than the paper strength may suggest.

Iraq's current and near-term military difficulties notwithstanding, it
would be shortsighted to dismiss its longer-term military potential to
threaten Gulf security if sanctions evaporate, the Iraqi economy rebounds,
it is able to acquire nuclear weapons, and Baghdad regains access to the
global arms market. Many readiness shortfalls could be corrected quickly

once its coffers start refilling. Furthermore, Iraq's active-duty military manpower is twice the size of combined Kuwaiti and Saudi armed forces. Of Iraq's 23 divisions, 6 are reasonably ready and well-armed Republican Guard units, and 6 others are armored or mechanized divisions of the regular Army. A SAM force of 1,500 launchers and 6,000 air defense guns gives Baghdad a reasonable capacity to defend Iraqi air space against moderate air threats. Although these weapons and equipment are no match for modern U.S. forces, they can be used effectively and provide a broad array of offensive options with which to menace Iraq's weaker neighbors, but not in the kind of massive armored offensives launched over a decade ago.

While public opinion focuses mainly on the prospect of another full-scale invasion of Kuwait and Saudi Arabia, Iraq has a range of limited military options at its disposal. For example, it could send large ground and air forces into the northern and southern no-fly zones to challenge U.S. enforcement of these arrangements; mount major military operations against the Kurds in the north and the Shiah resistance in the south; send forces into Jordan if that country's internal politics began to unravel; or conduct limited incursions into Kuwait, with ground and air strikes against oil fields, cities, and ports.

Nor is a major Iraqi invasion beyond the realm of imagination, especially in the absence of sizable U.S. forces. Although Baghdad would not commit its entire 23-division force to an operation against Kuwait and Saudi Arabia, due to competing demands, Iraq probably could pull together a force of 6 to 12 divisions, including 3 to 6 Republican Guard divisions and an equal number of armored and mechanized divisions from the regular army, in roughly 4 to 6 weeks if the erosion of sanctions allowed for some reconstitution of Iraq's logistical capabilities. If this force were skillfully used and accompanied by a deft political campaign that prevented U.S. reinforcement of the region, Iraq might be able to overrun large portions of Kuwait and Saudi Arabia. Iraq might accompany this attack with WMD and diplomatic threats in an effort to impede the arrival of U.S. reinforcements and intimidate other countries into denying support for U.S. military operations. Such an attack might not succeed in occupying all of Saudi Arabia, but overrunning Kuwait and part of the Saudi oil fields would deal a devastating blow to American interests and influence and require a major U.S. counteroffensive. If Iraq is able to acquire nuclear weapons, Saddam would be likely to threaten their use to preclude an American military response.

Iran

Over the last 10 years, Iran has made more progress than Iraq in compensating for the losses it sustained in a lost war (in this case, the Iran-Iraq War). Moreover, Iran has pursued a different approach to rebuilding its military and working within stringent constraints. Iran has had two major obstacles to overcome: the limited amount of money it has been able to devote to its military stemming from the poor state of its economy and the embargo on military sales to it by all of the Western states. As a result, Iran has had to be stingy with its weapons purchases and has largely had to buy from China, North Korea, and—when it wants to splurge—Russia (see table 4–2).

Given these circumstances, Tehran has spent its defense dollars reasonably well. It has developed a set of priorities and stuck to them. Iran has primarily focused its limited resources on antiship and antiair defenses in the Persian Gulf, particularly the Strait of Hormuz. Over the last 10 years, Iran has purchased CSS–2 Silkworm and CSS–3 Seersucker surface-launched antiship missiles, C–801 and C–802 sea- and air-launched antiship missiles, SA–5 SAMs, 3 *Kilo*-class diesel submarines, MiG–29 fighters, Su-24 attack aircraft, and large numbers of small fast-attack boats. Iran has also been diligent about training with these assets and appears to have acquired a reasonable degree of skill with them. Consequently, Tehran has acquired a modest sea denial capability in the Persian Gulf and the Strait of Hormuz that would be difficult for any nation other than the United States to overcome quickly, and even U.S. forces may only prevail with painful losses should Iran decide to close the Strait of Hormuz. Future Iranian acquisition of air and naval weapons, including

Table 4–2. **Iranian Military Forces, 1990–2001**

Category	1990	2001
Military personnel	500,000	573,000
Tanks	600	1,000
Other armored fighting vehicles	850	1,000
Artillery pieces	800	2,100
Combat aircraft	120	283
Major surface combatants	3	3
Minor surface combatants	75	220 +
Submarines	—	6

Source: International Institute for Strategic Studies, *The Military Balance, 1989–1990* and *The Military Balance, 2000–2001* (Oxford: Oxford University Press, 1989, 2000), and author's estimates.

missiles and mines, could increase the antiaccess/area denial threat facing the swift deployment of U.S. reinforcements in a crisis.

Iran has also invested heavily in its WMD programs and is pursuing four versions of its Shahab missile, with ranges from 900 to 3,500 miles. The launch of the Shahab-3 medium-range ballistic missile and the development of the Shahab-4 intermediate-range ballistic missile (IRBM) have marked out Iran's ballistic missile program as one of Tehran's highest priorities and an area where Iran is making significant progress. The Iranian nuclear program is only now recovering from 10 years of crippling mismanagement, and it also must overcome the rather stringent international sanctions against proliferation. If Iran receives assistance from Russia, Pakistan, China, or another nuclear state, however, this program could pick up speed quickly. Iran is known to possess both CW and BW agents, although it is not known whether it has weaponized them for delivery by ballistic missiles. If not, it is undoubtedly working to develop this capability.

Iran's conventional ground forces and the air forces that would support a ground war have received the least priority from Tehran and consequently have progressed little since the end of the Iran-Iraq War. Iran's equipment holdings have grown only modestly. Its most noteworthy acquisitions have been a few hundred T–72s and BMP–2s from a variety of former Warsaw Pact countries. However, this force is still a long way from fielding the thousands of modern armored fighting vehicles, artillery pieces, and support equipment with which it would want to fight a major land war against Iraq. Likewise, Iran has done little to acquire the kinds and numbers of aircraft it would need to support large ground forces in the field. Its largest acquisition of planes has actually been its effort to integrate the Iraqi fighters flown to Iran during the Gulf War into its own air forces. If successful, this integration would bring several dozen Mirage F–1s and Su-17/20/22 Fitters, along with additional Su-24s, into the Iranian order of battle. Tehran has done little else. Most noteworthy is the fact that they have not yet purchased large numbers of air superiority fighters (more MiG–29s or Su-27s) or dedicated ground support aircraft such as the Su-25, which will be crucial if Iran must again fight a major war with Iraq. In part, this has been a function of American efforts to prevent Russian arms sales to Iran, but to a greater extent, it has been because Tehran has simply preferred to put its resources into littoral defenses and weapons of mass destruction.

This allocation of resources reflects Iran's well-developed sense of threat priorities. At present, Iran feels most threatened by the United

States, second by Israel, third by Iraq, and last by Pakistan and its other land neighbors. The Iranians concluded that after the Gulf War, the Iraqis would remain flat on their backs and that the United States would keep them that way for some time. The power of the United States, on the other hand, is unchecked in the Gulf region, while Israel feels threatened by Iranian WMD programs and angered by Iran's continuing support of Hizballah, Hamas, and various Palestinian terrorist groups. Consequently, Tehran has put its resources into dealing with these threats: sea denial to try to prevent a U.S. attack on Iran from the Persian Gulf (or conceivably to shut off Persian Gulf oil exports as a source of leverage over the United States), and weapons of mass destruction to try to deter a U.S. or Israeli attack or to deter escalation if deterrence is unsuccessful. Because the Iranians see Iraq as more of a long-term threat, they have taken a "go-slow" approach toward rebuilding their ground and air forces. On the other hand, should the United States oust Saddam and replace him with a pro-American regime, Tehran might eventually decide that it does need to prepare for a major land war with Iraq, but the time required for Iraq to reconstitute a threat under such circumstances would be even longer than at present, and any U.S. occupation would presumably mean the termination of Iraqi WMD programs, at least for the time being. Nevertheless, the Iranians probably would still place their main emphasis on their own WMD efforts, seeing in nuclear weapons and ballistic missiles an asymmetric counter to the presence of U.S. forces in Iraq and, in the longer term, to the prospective threat of a resurgent U.S.-backed Iraq.

In the foreseeable future, Iran's threat perceptions are unlikely to change in any way that would fundamentally alter its military priorities. If economic sanctions on Iraq are lifted, this is unlikely to have more than a modest impact on Iraqi military power and is unlikely to spur Tehran suddenly to begin investing heavily in ground forces. Even if the military embargo is suspended (or is not enforced), Iraq would need at least 5, and probably more like 10, years to regain its pre-Gulf War strength. This too suggests that Iran can continue to take a slow, methodical approach to rebuilding its ground and air forces. Even in the event of a messy transition in Iraq with ensuing disorder and turmoil, Iran would probably seek to control the risk to itself indirectly, through manipulation of Iraqi client groups and the use of unconventional capabilities rather than with regular military forces. Only if Iran concluded that Iraq was close to acquiring a workable nuclear weapon would Iran feel significantly threatened, and in this case it would likely respond by accelerating its own nuclear program.

Consequently, we should expect Iran to continue to invest most heavily in WMD and sea denial forces. The key variable in determining how much progress Iran is able to make in these areas is how much foreign assistance the Iranians receive. If Iran receives fissile material, guidance equipment, and technical training from Pakistan or North Korea (or China or Russia, for that matter), its nuclear and ballistic missile programs might far exceed current estimates that Tehran is still roughly a decade away from having a nuclear device and a deployed IRBM fleet. Likewise, if Iran can get access to advanced Russian fighters such as the Su-27 Flanker, advanced air-to-air missiles such as the AA–12 Archer, advanced Russian SAMs such as the SA–10 Grumble or SA–12 Giant, and advanced Russian antiship missiles such as the SS–N–22 Sunburn, Iran's capabilities to defend the Persian Gulf littoral and deny access to the region to U.S. air and naval forces might increase dramatically.

Nevertheless, like Iraq, Iran too suffers from important intangible problems that ultimately are likely to place an upper limit on Iran's military growth over the next 10 years. The most visible of these is the severe interservice rivalry between the Islamic Revolutionary Guard Corps (IRGC) and Iran's regular armed services. The IRGC and the regulars compete for resources, missions, and prestige, and there is no love lost between them. Despite regime efforts to smooth cooperation by integrating their commands, relations between the IRGC and the regulars are very poor and have often led to bloodshed, even in recent years.

Interservice frictions are one element of the larger political problems that enshroud the Iranian military. Since Mohammed Khatami was elected president in 1997, Iranian society has been increasingly split between a sizable majority seeking democratic reforms of Iran's political, economic, and social systems and a minority tied to the current theocratic system. This split has created tensions throughout Iranian society and almost certainly has affected the armed forces as well. There is some limited evidence that the IRGC rank and file do not share the zealotry of their senior commanders, who remain among the most devoted adherents of clerical rule. Moreover, the regime looks to the IRGC to maintain domestic order and defend the establishment against internal threats. It is unclear how the IRGC rank and file would react or on whose side the Iranian regular armed forces would stand in the event of a popular uprising. All of these problems create uncertainty among Iran's leaders over how their forces will respond when called upon to act and erode the morale of the units themselves. Furthermore, the preferential treatment given to the IRGC probably has an adverse effect on morale and cooperation between regular military units and the IRGC.

Finally, even if Iranian forces were somehow able to overcome their political troubles and interservice frictions, they would still face considerable problems. Iranian forces have never been able to take full advantage of the equipment at their disposal. U.S. military officers who trained the Iranians before the 1979 revolution uniformly noted that the Iranians were not bad pilots, gunners, soldiers, and sailors, but they were not terrific ones either. This problem was highlighted during the Iran-Iraq War: the Iranians clearly were more effective than their clumsy Iraqi foes but still were not capable enough to take advantage of the constant opportunities the Iraqis presented them to score a decisive victory. Ultimately, the Iraqis managed to improve their effectiveness just enough to capitalize on their massive superiority in numbers, firepower, and chemical warfare and to defeat the Iranians. Today, Iranian forces, which have lost key U.S.-trained military personnel who fought against Iraq, may have a slight edge in military effectiveness over Iraqi forces but are far from Western or Israeli standards. Nonetheless, Iran possesses sufficient military capabilities to mount a stiff resistance to foreign invasion, including by U.S. forces. It does not represent, however, a serious threat of military invasion against its neighbors for the foreseeable future.

The Gulf Cooperation Council States

Since the Gulf War, the United States has striven mightily to improve the military capabilities of the GCC states. This effort has not been entirely fruitless, but the gains have been modest. The most noteworthy development has been the simple increase in the size of Saudi and Kuwaiti forces, especially in the categories of active manpower, heavy ground forces, and combat aircraft. A decade ago, the 2 countries were capable of fielding only 4.6 divisions and 215 combat aircraft; today, they field 8 divisions and 430 combat aircraft, an overall increase of about 85 percent in the size of their principal ground and air forces. Compared to Iraq, Saudi and Kuwaiti forces are outnumbered in manpower by about 2 to 1 and by ratios of 3 to 1 in divisions, 1.5 to 1 in tanks, and nearly 4 to 1 in artillery. In combat aircraft, the Saudis and Kuwaitis actually have a numerical edge of 430 to 316 (or a ratio of 1.36 to 1). Overall, the Iraqis now have an advantage of about 2 to 1 in numbers of troops and weapons, a considerable improvement over the nearly 10 to 1 advantage Baghdad enjoyed at the time of *Desert Storm.*

Two factors account for this narrowing of the numeric gap. First, Iraq's armed forces were slashed by more than one-half by *Desert Storm* and sanctions. Second, Saudi Arabia and Kuwait roughly doubled their forces. The expansion of Saudi and Kuwaiti air forces, coupled with the acquisition of Patriot missile batteries, is especially important because they probably now have enough aircraft to defend their skies against weak Iraqi opponents. However, Saudi and Kuwaiti ground forces remain undersized: only 8 division-equivalents and 544 artillery tubes.

Despite these improvements in Saudi and Kuwaiti forces over the past decade, the next 10 years may well witness an overall decline in GCC military capabilities relative to the projected modest growth in Iraqi and Iranian conventional capabilities (see table 4–3). At least for the moment, the bright spot in the GCC military firmament is Kuwait. Since the shock of the Iraqi invasion, Kuwait has gotten quite serious about its own defense, and this spirit has paid dividends. Kuwait has dedicated considerable assets to procurement and has acquired the equipment for a balanced, modern force: M1A2 tanks, M2 infantry fighting vehicles (IFVs), Patriot SAMs, F–18 fighters, and AH–64 attack helicopters. Of greater importance, Kuwaiti military personnel at all levels appear to have embraced the need to learn how to use this equipment to be able to defend their country. The Kuwaitis take their training seriously and are eager to improve their skills. As a result, Kuwaitis are already the most competent military in the Gulf (admittedly a low standard) and are slowly turning into a qualitatively respectable force by regional standards.

Table 4–3. **GCC Military Forces, 1990–2001**

Category	1990	2001
Military personnel	164,000	208,000
Tanks	1,200	1,800
Other armored fighting vehicles	2,300	4,600
Artillery pieces	1,100	1,500
Combat aircraft	300	590
Major surface combatants	8	9
Minor surface combatants	70	70
Submarines	—	—

Source: International Institute for Strategic Studies, *The Military Balance, 1989–1990* and *The Military Balance, 2000–2001* (Oxford: Oxford University Press, 1989, 2000).

Nevertheless, even if the Kuwaitis achieve Western standards of effectiveness with their superb weaponry 10 years from now, this will not rescue the GCC from military oblivion. Kuwait is simply too small to carry such a burden. Kuwait has an official population of 2.275 million. However, counting only male Kuwaiti citizens, the actual number is only 386,000, including old men and boys not eligible for military service.[2] This suggests that even if Kuwait were to turn itself into a new Sparta, with its entire eligible male populace devoted to military service or supporting the military, it probably could not field a force of more than 40,000 to 50,000 men in total—still inadequate, without U.S. assistance, against an Iraqi military that might boast over a half-million or even a million men at some point. Moreover, even if the Kuwaitis were able to field such a force as its contribution to a combined GCC force, the GCC states are not capable of standing up alone against Iraq.

While Kuwait's military seems to be improving slightly, Saudi Arabia's armed forces are deteriorating rapidly. The Kingdom has cut its military budget, and the crunch has hit operations, training, and maintenance hard. Even Saudi F–15 pilots have regressed from reasonable competence to mediocrity. Compounding these practical shortcomings is the lack of a warfighting doctrine. Without this foundation that spells out maneuver warfighting concepts, combined arms operations, or other sophisticated military skills, the Saudi armed forces will never realize the potential their high-tech weaponry promises.

It is unclear whether the Saudi military will pull out of its current decline any time soon. Riyadh faces deep-rooted economic and political problems that the long-term decline in oil prices has brought to the fore and that make military reform unlikely. Saudi Arabia's birthrate has soared, driving down per capita income and making the Kingdom's vast social welfare system a tremendous drain on the economy. Saudis no longer have the luxury of not working, but so far they have been unwilling to accept menial labor and other "lower-class" jobs, creating massive employment problems. The Saudi educational system is further exacerbating the problem by focusing principally on Islamic studies, law, and the humanities at the expense of science and mathematics. Every year, this system pumps out several hundred thousand new graduates, with few having the skills sought by the Kingdom's major industries. Moreover, military service, particularly in the land forces, is not a prestigious occupation and therefore fails to attract those graduates who are able to find higher status work or to live on family subsidies while unemployed.

Given these other priorities, Riyadh has clearly put military reform near the bottom of its list of priorities. This means that its impressive array of equipment—315 M1A2 tanks, 400 M–2 IFVs, 12 AH–64 attack helicopters, 160 F–15 fighters, 5 E–3 airborne warning and control system command aircraft—is unlikely to contribute much to the defense of the Arabian Peninsula. Nor is this situation likely to change dramatically in the near term. As long as Crown Prince Abdullah rules the Kingdom and (probably correctly) puts Saudi Arabia's massive demographic, economic, educational, political, and social problems first, the military is unlikely to be a priority for scarce resources that would allow the Saudis to enjoy military power commensurate with the weaponry they have acquired.

Although Saudi Arabia and Kuwait possess large numbers of modern weapons, this does not mean that they can use them effectively. Combat proficiency is influenced by many qualitative factors, and the Iraqis, despite their own weaknesses, have a distinct edge in several of them. Nonetheless, some qualitative considerations weigh in favor of the Saudis and Kuwaitis. This is especially true, for example, in the air, where both countries operate more modern combat aircraft and train more effectively than their Iraqi counterparts. If the Saudi and Kuwaiti qualitative advantage on the ground is less decisive, their 675 M–1 tanks and 400 Bradley IFVs are far better than Iraq's best armor.

There are, in addition, other constraints on the operational effectiveness of Saudi and Kuwaiti forces. Most notably, their forces are not integrated into a single military command, and their military establishments lack the capacity to coordinate multi-unit, joint, and combined arms operations on a large scale. Because the GCC commitment to collective defense lacks the kind of automaticity embodied in the North Atlantic Treaty Organization Article 5 commitment, the Saudis (and other GCC countries) might respond to an Iraqi invasion of Kuwait not by rushing to Kuwait's rescue but instead by preparing to defend their own borders, making Iraq's military task far easier. If both countries do not reverse the trend of reduced force modernization and readiness, the gap with Iraq will start to widen and could accelerate rapidly if Baghdad manages to get out from under international sanctions.

The forces of the other four GCC states also deserve mention. Collectively, they add up to 132,000 troops, 4.7 division equivalents, and 193 combat aircraft. Still, whether these forces would actually be committed and fight effectively against an Iraqi attack on Kuwait and Saudi Arabia remains very much in doubt. Over the last 10 years, Bahrain, the United

Arab Emirates (UAE), Oman, and Qatar have acquired some impressive weapons systems. The UAE has 80 new, cutting-edge F–16 fighters that could prove to be a capable force. However, individual weapons systems do not equal actual military power, and none of the Gulf states has the full panoply of combat and combat support systems required to fight and win modern wars. Even taken as a whole (and this would require a degree of integration in command, training, doctrine, and communications that they have hitherto been unwilling or unable to adopt), the forces of the smaller GCC states do not add up to a modern military. Only the Saudis have the resources to field a fully capable military, to which the other GCC states could contribute their own unique niche capabilities. However, as noted above, the Saudis never reached the standard when defense was a priority, and today they are falling further from this mark. In addition, it remains uncertain whether the smaller GCC states are prepared to occupy their own niches, since all of them tend to see each other as potential rivals. On the other hand, some recent ventures in GCC-wide defense cooperation—principally the Hizam al-Tawwun combined air command, control, and communications project, which provides radars, early warning, and secure communications links—bode well for future cooperation.

The bottom line is that Saudi Arabia, Kuwait, and the other GCC states are unlikely to become militarily self-sufficient against the Iraqi threat during the next decade and possibly beyond. But they have made some progress over the past decade in improving their military capabilities, and U.S. efforts to push them further in this direction—or at least to avoid further slippage—should be pursued. Perhaps more importantly, military self-sufficiency is an unrealistic and inappropriate standard to apply in judging the adequacy of Gulf state military capabilities, since their forces are only expected to perform in conjunction with a U.S coalition. In this context, the more capable the Gulf states are in contributing to a staunch forward defense, even if it is a matter of adding only a couple of days, the better the prospects for rapid U.S. deployment of forces to the Gulf and decisive military operations. How this goal can best be accomplished is addressed in chapter five.

Egypt

On paper, as shown in table 4–4, Egypt possesses a formidable arsenal that will only grow over the next few years. By 2004, Egypt will possess 750 M1A1 tanks, 175 M109 self-propelled howitzers, 225 F–16 fighters, 36 AH–64 Apache attack helicopters, 5 E–2C airborne command aircraft, and

Table 4–4. **Egyptian Military Forces, 1990–2001**

Category	1990	2001
Military personnel	450,000	450,000
Tanks	2,400	3,100
Other armored fighting vehicles	3,700	5,000
Artillery pieces	1,200	1,200
Combat aircraft	510	580
Major surface combatants	6	11
Minor surface combatants	43	40
Submarines	10	4

Source: International Institute for Strategic Studies, *The Military Balance, 1989–1990* and *The Military Balance, 2000–2001* (Oxford: Oxford University Press, 1989, 2000).

4 *Oliver Hazard Perry*–class frigates. However, financial, political, and bureaucratic problems, coupled with severe shortcomings in military effectiveness, suggest that Egypt's military power may actually *decline* over the next 5 to 10 years despite its new ultramodern weapons.

The most obvious problem plaguing the Egyptian military is underfunding. In 1999, Egypt spent $2.5 billion on defense (less than 1 percent of GDP) while receiving another $2.1 billion in foreign military assistance from the United States. This is woefully inadequate to meet the needs of an army of nearly a half-million men. In 1997, the latest year for which information is available, Egypt ranked 97th in the world in terms of military spending per capita (right behind Swaziland) and 130th in the world in terms of military spending per soldier (after Mozambique).[3] As a result, Egypt must cut corners constantly—particularly with regard to training and maintenance. Egyptian air force bases often have only a few hundred dollars a month to conduct training and maintenance, meaning that pilots log relatively few hours in the air and generally are not allowed to practice even with bomb-demonstration units let alone live ordnance. However, part of the problem is also a misallocation of the available funding. In particular, Cairo insists on purchasing ever more new equipment at the expense of funding the training and maintenance needed actually to employ the equipment it already has. Indeed, the United States has urged the Egyptians for over a decade to cut back on procurement of new weapons in favor of training, maintenance, and logistics. In recent years, they have had some success, as Egypt has agreed to spend roughly 30 percent of the military aid it receives from the United States on logistics and maintenance, but this is still a far cry from a proper balance. As a result, roughly half of Egypt's fleet of F–16s is nonoperational at any given time, and similar problems afflict the navy and army.

The Egyptian military also remains deeply politicized, further hindering performance. Advancement for senior officers increasingly is predicated on political connections, particularly ties to President Hosni Mubarak. Graft is rampant. Many senior officers have carved out independent fiefdoms within the services, while the rivalries among the services are so severe that joint operations are effectively nonexistent. A particularly troublesome manifestation of these problems is an extreme compartmentalization of information at all levels of the Egyptian chain of command. Officers are unwilling to provide information to their colleagues to ensure their own continued importance, to their subordinates to maintain control over them, and to their superiors for fear of betraying information that could reflect badly on them.

The Egyptian armed forces also live in a torpor common to most Egyptian bureaucracies. Between 1967 and 1973, the shame of defeat by Israel in the Six-Day War injected great energy into the Egyptian armed forces. This sense of mission allowed Egypt to overcome various bureaucratic impediments and to create a more efficient military. Today, this sense of purpose is effectively gone. Most Egyptian officers understandably see few external threats to the country and therefore no reason to try to make the system work better. The result is a rigid hierarchy that makes every request a nightmare and contributes to the glacial pace and generally low morale of the Egyptian armed forces.

Finally, Egypt's armed forces continue to suffer from a number of debilitating problems of military ineffectiveness that thoroughly undermine Egyptian military power. Over the last 60 years, passive and unimaginative tactical leadership has bedeviled Egyptian forces. Egyptian personnel, especially their junior field officers, have little understanding of maneuver warfare or combined arms operations (even within each service). Their pilots are extremely poor, and only a handful can handle basic fighter maneuvers, let alone advanced combat maneuvering. Egyptian personnel often have limited technical skills (many enlisted personnel still come to the armed forces illiterate), and colonels and brigadier generals often must do the work that lieutenants and captains in Western militaries would do because they are the only ones with the technical know-how to handle sophisticated gear. Egypt's F–16 pilots have little ability to take advantage of the capabilities of the aircraft. For this reason, the greater sophistication of

Egypt's weapons should not be equated with corresponding improvements in military capability, since so few of their personnel can employ the equipment. Indeed, one reason Cairo shies away from dissimilar training between its F–16 and MiG–21 squadrons is that the MiG is so much simpler that its pilots are more proficient with it and they fear that the "elite" F–16s might get shown up by their MiGs.

Also, the Egyptian military culture makes it extremely difficult to overcome these problems. For example, the oppressive fear of incurring shame in Arab society means that Egyptian military units, like their Arab counterparts elsewhere in the region, rarely ever debrief after a mission or critique their performances. As a result, the same mistakes are repeated again and again. This is the single biggest problem the Egyptians face in trying to improve their military effectiveness. Overlaid on this cultural disposition is an antiquated and inflexible command and control system. In part because they cannot rely on independent leadership from their tactical commanders and in part because of their predilection for top-down management, the Egyptians also rely on minutely scripted set-piece operations that are outmoded in an era of rapidly moving maneuver battles that take place simultaneously on the ground and in the air—serious deficiencies against sophisticated and well-armed opponents. In the words of one officer, "The Egyptians put an inordinate effort into tremendously detailed planning, but if the situation changes, they are not capable of adapting their plans to the changed circumstances."

Egypt seems unlikely to address these problems any time soon. In the twilight of the Mubarak era, there are few voices calling for change. The military is largely complacent; there is no great threat that might energize a reform effort. The society is preoccupied with economic problems and their concomitant social disruptions. Indeed, many in the military are more concerned with maintaining their privileged position in society than with undertaking a painful reform process to improve their military capabilities. Despite billions of dollars of U.S. assistance over the years, Egypt's forces are still largely saddled with obsolete equipment and an inflexible organization and doctrine. Even if U.S. aid continues at current levels (hardly a sure bet), using that money effectively to make the Egyptian military a modern force would require downsizing and reallocating resources as well as changing patterns of behavior. Given economic realities, however, downsizing is a non-starter because of the effect on unemployment. Meanwhile, the political clout of the officer corps demands that they be placated by resources and acquisition of prestige equipment, digging the hole even deeper for the armed forces.

Egypt's performance during *Desert Storm* demonstrated the results of all of these problems. Cairo could not get its forces to Saudi Arabia without U.S. lift. It could not supply those forces once they were there without American logistics. It could not plan or direct its forces without U.S. assistance. And its forces performed poorly in actual combat operations, failing to achieve any of their objectives and leaving the flanks of both the U.S. Marine Corps and U.S. Army advances vulnerable.

The saving grace for Egypt may be that all the other regional militaries, with the obvious exception of Israel's, suffer from these same deficiencies to a greater or lesser extent. Unfortunately, both Cairo and Washington expect the Egyptian armed forces to play a regional role that it cannot fulfill unless it transcends the lowest common denominator of Arab military proficiency. The trend line for the next 10 years would suggest that the United States should not expect the Egyptian military to live up to these expectations unless Washington and Cairo can agree on a serious understanding of and commitment to the role of the Egyptian armed forces in regional security. Failing that, it will be difficult to shake the cobwebs loose in Cairo and convince the Egyptian high command to undertake a comprehensive reform that few seem to see a need for.

Jordan

If the United States can count on only very modest help from its Gulf allies and Egypt, it should expect virtually none from Jordan due to political, military, financial, and demographic factors. As indicated in table 4–5, Jordan's armed forces remain very small and fairly weak. They are roughly half the size of the combined GCC military and, more importantly, operate far fewer modern weapons. Of 1,250 tanks, only about 300 are new British Challengers. Of 106 combat aircraft, only 16 are F–16s. The root of this problem is Jordan's faltering economy, which has realized little gain from peace with Israel and faces a population (particularly a Palestinian population) that is growing far beyond the ability of the economy to absorb. These economic problems not only limit procurement, but they also constrain training, maintenance, deployments, and logistical support. In 1997, Jordanian military expenditures per soldier ranked 117th in the world.[4]

On the positive side, the Jordanian armed forces still retain some of the vestiges of the old Arab Legion created by the British, which gives

Table 4–5. Jordanian Military Forces, 1990–2001

Category	1990	2000
Military personnel	85,000	103,000
Tanks	1,150	1,250
Other armored fighting vehicles	1,400	1,500
Artillery pieces	250	550
Combat aircraft	110	106
Major surface combatants	—	—
Minor surface combatants	—	6
Submarines	—	—

Source: International Institute for Strategic Studies, *The Military Balance, 1989–1990* and *The Military Balance, 2000–2001* (Oxford: Oxford University Press, 1989, 2000).

Jordanian units generally higher levels of military effectiveness than most of their Arab brethren. In particular, the Jordanian armed forces remain about 85 percent volunteer, and most volunteers remain in the service for many years. As a result of the professional tradition established by the British, morale, discipline, and proficiency among Jordanian soldiers and officers tend to be higher than in most of the Arab armies. Indeed, during the 1980s, Iraq used Jordanian instructors to teach its fighter pilots. The caliber and professionalism of the Jordanians are higher—especially higher in the Jordanian military hierarchy. That said, quality varies widely from unit to unit, with the Royal Jordanian Air Force, Royal Guard, and Special Forces near the top and other units at the bottom.

Additionally, the Jordanians suffer from many of the debilitating problems of military ineffectiveness as the other Arab armies. Jordanian tactical commanders are often reluctant to show initiative or develop innovative approaches to solving battlefield problems and have difficulty adapting to unforeseen events. They rely on heavily scripted exercises, prefer to defer decisionmaking to higher levels of command, and often have difficulty making combined arms operations work properly. Although better than most regional militaries, many Jordanian personnel find it difficult to take full advantage of what little sophisticated hardware is in the inventory. Likewise, information does not always flow smoothly up, down, or across the Jordanian command structure to those who need it most.

Due to the limits on their military effectiveness, their small size, and their budgetary constraints, Jordan would be hard pressed to defend itself against a full-scale Iraqi (or Syrian) invasion and would be quickly overcome by the Israel Defense Force in any potential operation. Consequently, a deployment to the Gulf of more than token forces would likely be too much for Jordan's limited military capabilities, assuming it were even politically possible for Jordan to take up arms against Iraq. It appears likely, however, that Jordan would provide limited support to a U.S. military invasion of Iraq.

Conclusion

It is illusory to believe that the GCC countries will ever acquire the capacity to defend themselves against large-scale aggression without U.S. military intervention. Nonetheless, the near-term trends in the regional military balance appear favorable to the United States, as long as we continue to devote significant military resources to the Persian Gulf. Furthermore, Gulf state forces, if they were able to overcome the most serious constraints on their military effectiveness, could help to complicate and delay an Iraqi attack and support the arrival of American reinforcements.

These conclusions may seem counterintuitive at first glance. Iraq and Iran appear likely to enhance their overall capabilities, further climbing out of the troughs resulting from their defeats during the Iran-Iraq War (for Iran) and the Gulf War (for Iraq). At the same time, the capabilities of U.S. allies in the region—the GCC states, Egypt, and Jordan—may not keep pace with Iran or Iraq. Indeed, the military gains Saudi Arabia made over the past decade could be erased in the coming years due to declining oil revenues and military expenditures, shifting threat perceptions, and the lower emphasis the Saudi royal family (and other GCC leaders) is placing on military preparedness to instead address ultimately more dire economic, political, and social problems.

In the near term, both of these potential trends are ultimately irrelevant because the increase in Iraqi and Iranian capabilities is likely to be modest. Even when combined with a possible decline in the military capabilities of the moderate Arab states, they do not threaten to reverse the current regional military balance. Moreover, anticipated improvements in Iraqi and Iranian capabilities are likely to pale in comparison with the dramatic advances expected in U.S. capabilities during the same period. In short, the favorable military balance of today is likely to tilt even further in U.S. favor for at least the next 5 years and possibly beyond. Moreover, these positive trends appear quite strong. None are based on the whims of idiosyncratic leaders, but instead on powerful demographic, economic, political, social, and cultural factors.

Nevertheless, barring fundamental changes in the character and intentions of the regimes in Iraq and Iran, several trends could converge some time in the latter part of this decade to upset the regional military balance. First, the huge international coalition that the United States assembled during the Gulf War has dissipated, and putting it back together will be difficult in the absence of a clear and present Iraqi danger. Second, military sanctions on the current Iraqi regime and Iran will continue to erode and may disappear altogether, allowing both countries to purchase increasing quantities of sophisticated weaponry and to correct other serious military shortcomings. Third, both Iran and Iraq are likely to acquire weapons of mass destruction and particularly nuclear weapons to underwrite their geopolitical ambitions. Finally, the United States will face increasing difficulties in sustaining its military presence in the region and in overcoming the challenges to its force projection capabilities arising from growing Iraqi and Iranian antiaccess/area denial capabilities.

Together, these countervailing trends suggest that American friends and allies in the Persian Gulf will remain vulnerable to Iraqi and Iranian military capabilities and that only U.S. military power can maintain a stable regional military balance. However, as discussed in the following chapter, maintaining this favorable regional military balance requires substantial reinforcements from the United States and thus runs counter to the new U.S. global defense strategy. Thus, the long-term dynamics of the regional force balance underscore the importance of reexamining U.S. defense strategy, military requirements, and force planning for the Persian Gulf and concepts for transforming the forces of America's Gulf state allies.

Notes

[1] The assessment in this chapter of the future military balance between Iraq and the Gulf states assumes that the regime of Saddam Husayn will remain in power for the foreseeable future. This assumption should not be construed as an endorsement of the policy of containment. To the contrary, the assessment of the regional military balance, which is based on a straight-line projection of the current geopolitical order, clearly illustrates the long-term dangers of allowing Saddam to remain in power. It also reflects the difficulty of analyzing regional military dynamics in light of the considerable uncertainties about the impact of U.S. military operations on Iraqi military capabilities, the nature of a post-Saddam Iraqi government, and the kind of arrangements that might be put in place in a post-Saddam transition to limit the size and capabilities of the Iraqi armed forces. Because of the large number of possible permutations, an assessment of the implications of regime change in Iraq for the regional military balance would have little practical value.

[2] International Institute for Strategic Studies, *The Military Balance 2000–2001* (Oxford: Oxford University Press, 2000).

[3] United States Arms Control and Disarmament Agency, *World Military Expenditures and Arms Transfers, 1998* (Washington, DC: Government Printing Office, April 2000).

[4] Ibid.

Chapter Five

U.S. Defense Strategy and Force Planning

Richard L. Kugler

The idea that large American forces should be committed to defense of the Persian Gulf has become a staple of modern American defense planning in the post-Cold War world. Because the Persian Gulf will remain volatile and threatened, this strategic reality seems unlikely to change any time soon. But the future will not permit current U.S. defense plans there to remain static. Indeed, pressures for change are building as a result of developments in both Gulf security affairs and U.S. global defense strategy, and they seem destined to intensify in the coming period.

These pressures for change are giving rise to two key issues. The most visible and controversial issue is the footprint of the normal U.S. peacetime presence in the Persian Gulf: whether it should decrease, increase, or mutate in response to new geopolitical crosscurrents that are pulling in opposite directions. A less visible but equally important issue is whether and how changes should be made in the large American-based reinforcements that not only would swiftly deploy to the Gulf in the event of major war there but also that are needed for important purposes elsewhere. Exactly how these issues will be resolved remains to be seen, but the U.S. peacetime presence and wartime military commitment there likely will be significantly different in 5 or 10 years than they are today, with or without regime change in Iraq. In order to shape the future rather than be victimized by it, U.S. defense plans and forces for the Persian Gulf will need to transform in a way that reflects the larger changes sweeping the entire military establishment and its overseas operations. Carrying out this transition wisely in ways that take hold in the Gulf will be a key endeavor facing U.S. defense strategy and foreign policy because it will influence not only U.S. interests and goals there but also the ability of U.S. forces to carry out new missions in other regions.

Regime change in Iraq and other favorable developments may lessen the challenges of defending American interests in the Persian Gulf. Even with a change, however, U.S. defense plans face a demanding future. This chapter does not offer a fixed blueprint for how the United States should respond. Instead, its aim is to analyze the emerging trends, issues, and options in hope of illuminating the main factors that will influence the choices ahead. The analysis begins by examining the current U.S. military commitments to the Persian Gulf, with respect to both routine peacetime presence and wartime reinforcement plans. Drawing on the assessment of the regional force balance in the preceding chapter, it then examines how U.S. military requirements and force planning for the region will be affected by changes occurring in U.S. global defense strategy and transformation priorities, as articulated in the 2001 *Quadrennial Defense Review Report* (*QDR Report*). Finally, it addresses alternatives for designing the future U.S. peacetime presence and wartime reinforcement plans in ways that make sense not only in the Persian Gulf but also for future force operations along the entire southern strategic arc of instability.

Current Persian Gulf Defense Plans

The importance of the Persian Gulf to U.S. strategic interests is beyond question. Whereas the region already produces fully 45 percent of the world's oil, it likely will produce up to 60 percent a decade or two from now. While the United States draws only a small portion of its oil from the Gulf, other regions, including Europe and Asia, are more heavily dependent. Many countries, including the United States, are trying to develop alternative sources of oil and to conserve on energy consumption but thus far with modest success. The enduring reality is that an adequate worldwide supply at fair-market prices will remain reliant on unfettered access to Gulf oil. Beyond this, weapons of mass destruction (WMD) proliferation and other new-era geopolitical dynamics mean that a volatile Gulf region will have ripple effects elsewhere, triggering broader instabilities and dangers as globalization accelerates. In important ways, a stable Gulf will be needed in order to create stable security affairs in other endangered regions.

Military power, of course, is not the only instrument for pursuing U.S. goals in the Persian Gulf; indeed, diplomacy and multilateral economic policies are probably more important. But in a region where physical muscle still matters greatly in more ways than one, military power remains an important instrument and an ultimate court of last resort. For this reason alone, no sensible analyst would question the premise that U.S.

military strategy should continue to make ample provision for defending the Gulf, our allies there, and our access to its oil. The challenge lies in translating this premise into a concrete defense plan and force posture that reliably will get the job done. Meeting this challenge has not been easy in the past, and it does not promise to get easier in the future.

The Historical Legacy

If the proverbial Man from Mars were to survey current U.S. defense plans for the Persian Gulf, he would be puzzled by their apparent inconsistency. On the one hand, the routine U.S. peacetime military presence there is relatively small: normally about 20,000 to 25,000 military personnel. This presence is far less than the 100,000 troops deployed in both Europe and Asia and seems oddly limited for a region that is widely regarded as one of the most strategically important, geopolitically volatile, and war-endangered on Earth. On the other hand, the current ambitious wartime plan to dispatch a huge portion of the U.S. military posture to defend against an Iraqi invasion of Kuwait seems equally odd, since the enemy presumably being fought is not a rival superpower but a medium-sized country of 23 million people with a mostly outdated military that was crushed in the Gulf War a decade ago. How is it that the United States finds itself today in this curious position of committing forces that seemingly are so few in peacetime and so many in wartime?

History, local politics, and cultural and religious sensitivities largely account for this situation. Had purely military calculations dominated, the U.S. peacetime presence in the Gulf likely would have been significantly larger than actually became the case. But these sensitivities made a big day-to-day presence unpalatable. Accordingly, the United States elected to maintain a relatively modest (in comparison with other regions) presence that could perform important missions yet might not be fully adequate for deterrence and initial defense on its own. This step, in turn, compelled U.S. strategists to configure a large, highly visible, and credible reinforcement posture that could be swiftly rushed to the scene in time to gain control of any impending crisis.

Peacetime Presence

The routine U.S. military presence in the Persian Gulf is a variable, not a constant. (Except where indicated, the following discussion of the future U.S. peacetime presence in the Gulf region does not take into account the American forces deployed there over the past several months for possible military action against Iraq.) As of early 2002, about 60,000 troops were deployed across the U.S. Central Command (CENTCOM) area, including Afghanistan and its vicinity. In any single month, the number in the Gulf varies as a function of the ebb and flow of U.S. Air Force units and whether a carrier battlegroup (CVBG) and an amphibious ready group (ARG) are both on station. When only one of them is present, the number drops to under 20,000. In order to perform training exercises, units from the continental United States (CONUS) are temporarily deployed, thereby surging the number of personnel above the normal level.

Contrary to popular impressions, the routine U.S. military presence is not concentrated in Saudi Arabia. Indeed, only about 11,000 U.S. troops are normally stationed ashore in the entire Gulf region, with the remaining 10,000 to 14,000 deployed at sea aboard a CVBG and an ARG that carries marine ground and air forces. Of the ashore forces, about 5,110 are typically based in Saudi Arabia; 4,690 are located in Kuwait; and the remainder are scattered in small numbers among Bahrain, Oman, Qatar, and the United Arab Emirates (UAE). Principal U.S. military headquarters are the CENTCOM joint operations center at Prince Sultan Air Base near Riyadh, Saudi Arabia, and Fifth Fleet Headquarters at Manama, Bahrain. While Saudi Arabia remains an important anchor of the U.S. military presence in the Gulf, the biggest news in recent years is the extent to which U.S. personnel and forces are shifting to Kuwait, Qatar, and other Gulf Cooperation Council (GCC) countries.

The principal U.S. combat presence in the Gulf is air power provided by the Air Force and the Navy. The Air Force stations about 6,600 personnel and the equivalent of one fighter wing (60 to 70 aircraft: F–15s, F–16s, and A–10s), backed by various support aircraft including airborne warning and control systems and joint surveillance and target attack radar systems (JSTARS), which are divided among bases in Saudi Arabia and Kuwait. The Navy CVBG provides an additional wing of combat and support aircraft; the afloat Marine Corps force provides a few additional aircraft. The Army presence is small: only about 3,400 troops that operate a Patriot air defense battalion and a few additional infantry units that provide advisory services to allied forces, perform logistic support functions, and help populate headquarters staffs. The Army also deploys prepositioned equipment for two heavy brigades in Kuwait and Qatar, backed by another brigade set of equipment afloat on ships. These three prepositioned brigade sets, coupled with a Marine brigade-sized equipment set on ships at Diego Garcia, give the Department of Defense (DOD) the capacity to deploy a reinforced division swiftly without having to station the roughly 50,000 combat and support troops permanently that normally would be needed to operate this equipment.

The size and composition of this peacetime presence is partly a product of daily military requirements for performing ongoing missions. The U.S. headquarters staffs provide assets for establishing an influential U.S. presence, monitoring the situation, administering security assistance, and preparing crisis plans. The combat posture of an Air Force fighter wing, a Navy CVBG and ARG, and three Army prepositioned brigades provides units to carry out Operation *Southern Watch*, train with allied forces, establish a credible deterrent, and perform initial combat operations in the early stages of a war before reinforcements can arrive. This presence, however, is also partly a product of political constraints that keep its size below what might otherwise be the case. Although Saudi Arabia and other Gulf allies attach considerable importance to U.S. security guarantees, they prefer to keep the U.S. military footprint on their soil as small as possible because of its negative impact on their domestic politics. While these countries typically deny press reports that they want U.S. forces to depart, none of them are beating the drums for stationing larger forces on their soil.

This continuing military presence in the Gulf is a mixed blessing for the United States; while it serves important strategic purposes, it also imposes added demands on already-taxed U.S. force operations worldwide. For U.S. military personnel, Gulf duty is more difficult than tours in Europe and Northeast Asia, where the climate and other conditions are more amenable to their normal lives. Today's presence of up to 25,000 personnel is only 2 percent of the DOD total active military manpower, but when added to the larger forces that are deployed in Europe and Asia, it raises overseas presence to about 235,000 troops, or 17 percent of the total. The impact intensifies the strains placed on DOD readiness, manpower policies, and operations budgets. Indeed, the Air Force is compelled to station nearly one-third of its active combat units overseas, and the Navy is unable to keep three CVBGs and three ARGs constantly stationed abroad in the Mediterranean, the western Pacific, and the Gulf. With today's force levels and regional commitments elsewhere, DOD would be hard pressed to sustain for a prolonged period a vastly bigger Persian Gulf presence even if the opportunity presented itself.

Owing to these political and operational constraints, the principal feature of the normal U.S. peacetime presence is its relatively small size, not its allegedly big footprint. The strategic stakes and risks inherent in Gulf security affairs seemingly create a rationale for a larger presence. By comparison, for example, the United States deploys 37,000 troops in South Korea backed by another 38,000 troops in nearby Japan in order to safeguard deterrence on the Korean Peninsula. Thus far, the routine Gulf presence has proven to be strategically effective because it is structured efficiently, with a larger number of Air Force and Navy air combat forces than normally would be the case for this small amount of manpower. Headquarters staffs are kept lean to reduce the total. In addition, the reliance on prepositioned Army equipment rather than fully manned units reduces the U.S. military presence by fully 30,000 troops or more. If headquarters staffs were larger and the 3 Army brigades were fully manned, the normal U.S. presence likely would rise to about 60,000 to 65,000 troops. The bottom line is that the U.S. Persian Gulf presence may complicate political relationships there and strain DOD global operations, but it also buys alliance reassurance, deterrence, and initial defense on the cheap.

Wartime Reinforcements

History, strategy, and recent military requirements also explain the size and nature of the large reinforcement posture DOD earmarked for a major Gulf crisis. After the Gulf War of 1991, the Bush administration embarked upon a major downsizing (about 20 percent) of the large Cold War-era force posture. Crafting a regional defense strategy to replace the global strategy of the Cold War, it created a Base Force of 15 Army and Marine active divisions, 26 Air Force active and reserve fighter wings, 12 CVBGs, and 435 ships. The major drawdown, however, came in forces previously allocated to Europe and the North Atlantic Treaty Organization (NATO), not Asia or the Persian Gulf. In Europe, the U.S. peacetime presence dropped from 330,000 troops to 150,000. In Asia, the U.S. commitment to South Korea and Japan was mostly unchanged. In the Persian Gulf, the defeat of Iraq meant that DOD would no longer have to deploy the huge *Desert Storm* posture required for the wartime defense of Kuwait and containment of Iraq. But a still-sizable reinforcement plan was needed to safeguard against the risk that Iraq might rebuild its forces to some degree and use them to launch another war of aggression.

When the Clinton administration arrived in 1993, it pursued another downsizing of U.S. forces (a further 10 to 15 percent cutback) by deciding upon a reduced posture of 13 Army and Marine divisions, 20 Air Force fighter wings, 11 to 12 CVBGs, and about 350 ships. It also created a new defense strategy that called for DOD to prepare to wage two major regional conflicts in overlapping time frames. Because Europe no longer was seen as a theater likely to produce a major war (troop levels there were further reduced to 100,000), Northeast Asia and the Persian Gulf became the principal focal points of force planning. This emphasis on fighting two concurrent wars was reaffirmed in the DOD *Quadrennial Defense Review* of 1997, which continued the focus on two major theater wars (MTWs): a Korean war and a Gulf war against Iraq. Throughout the Clinton era, the DOD use of this two-MTW strategy as a force-sizing tool led to the judgment that about one-half of the U.S. conventional force posture should be allocated to each conflict. As a result, Persian Gulf plans took possession of a large joint posture of up to 7 Army and Marine divisions, 10 fighter wings, and 4 to 5 deployable CVBGs. CENTCOM was authorized to develop operation plans accordingly, with a wartime deployment scheme that began with small flexible deployment options and progressed upward eventually to include this entire posture.

Throughout the Clinton era, professional military judgment held that a joint posture of this large size could be required to wage another Gulf war against Iraq. The reason was not only to stop another Iraqi invasion, but also to launch subsequently a decisive counterattack aimed at restoring allied borders and occupying Iraq itself. The growing importance of Gulf plans in U.S. defense strategy, however, went well beyond this theory of wartime requirements. Along with an MTW in Korea, the goal of being prepared to wage a Gulf MTW against Iraq became a sine qua non for shaping the entire DOD force structure, program, and budget—and for justifying them to the Congress and public. In this atmosphere, a widespread consensus grew that these large forces should be earmarked for a new Gulf war and should not be regarded as readily available for use in any other conflicts, especially in other regions. DOD policy proclaimed that exceptions could be made for such pressing events as the Kosovo war and major peacekeeping missions—but with the stipulation that any Gulf-oriented forces used for these purposes must be capable of being promptly extracted and sent to the Gulf if a crisis erupted there. This policy applied to both Gulf-earmarked forces in CONUS and U.S. forces stationed in Europe, most of which were assigned to Gulf reinforcement plans despite also being committed to NATO defense roles. The effect was to solidify Gulf defense plans and elevate them to a position of commanding importance in DOD programming and budgeting, but at the expense of rigidly committing nearly one-half of the U.S. force posture to the point where it was no longer a flexible instrument for use elsewhere.

By the end of the 1990s, U.S. defense strategy for the Persian Gulf thus had completed its decade-long evolutionary march to produce the situation of today. Unlike the 1980s, the United States now stations significant forces in the Persian Gulf in peacetime. But owing to the region's political constraints, this routine presence is relatively small—much less than called for by the standards normally employed in other regions for a viable deterrent and initial defense force. To help compensate for this weakness, U.S. defense strategy for waging a Gulf war depends greatly upon swiftly deploying reinforcements from CONUS. In marked contrast to the small peacetime presence, the joint posture currently assigned to this reinforcement role is large and well-armed: about two-thirds the size of the *Desert Storm* force, even though today's Iraqi threat is only one-half the size of the 1990 threat.

This large reinforcement posture is not necessarily oversized in relation to the wartime requirements that could arise in the Gulf. Yet it is decidedly stronger than the forces of our allies and, provided it can be deployed on time, seems readily capable of rebuffing any aggressive threat that Iraq could mount today or of decisively defeating Iraqi forces and occupying Baghdad and the rest of the country. Equally important, it consumes a large portion of the total U.S. military posture, up to 50 percent of forces that are needed to carry out a global defense strategy, including in other endangered regions. The strategic benefit of this large reinforcement posture has been heightened security and stability in the Gulf. But because this posture is so large and so rigidly committed, the result is less flexibility for other wartime missions and potentially less security in other regions as well.

Impact of New U.S. Defense Strategy

Irrespective of how much progress local friends and allies make in improving their military capabilities, the Persian Gulf seems destined to remain a geopolitical hot zone with an unstable military balance that, unless regime change occurs in Iraq, will tempt Iraq (and possibly other potential adversaries) to throw their weight around and even to resort to aggression. Danger lies ahead because some military trends, notably WMD proliferation, are growing worse. As a result, the United States will face the necessity of firmly and steadily applying its military power there for the foreseeable future. But today's political and military setting differs greatly from that of a decade ago, and a decade from now, the setting likely will differ appreciably from today. The proper approach to designing an appropriate future American peacetime presence and wartime commitment is to act in ways that not only respond to future trends but also can help shape them in a manner that advances U.S. and allied interests. Thus, U.S. defense strategy and forces for the Gulf need to be proactive, not merely reactive—and they need to change with the times.

Any attempt to address future U.S. defense strategy in the Persian Gulf is clouded by uncertainty about the future of Iraq and by other regional trends. If the United States and other partners are successful in removing Saddam from power, much will depend upon the new regime that rules Iraq in the aftermath. In the event that Saddam is replaced by a stable and peaceful pro-American regime, the United States likely will face fewer enduring military requirements in the Persian Gulf than it does now. Moreover, most of these needs would probably be best met by a mix of forward-deployed forces that was dominated more by air and naval than ground forces, creating the opportunity in turn for a presence that has more of an expeditionary rather than a permanent and occupational character. A less attractive prospect is that Iraq is plunged into a period of prolonged chaos, thereby necessitating military occupation by the United States and its allies in an environment that has been destabilized and radicalized by American military intervention. A worse prospect is that Saddam is replaced by a new regime that still has nationalist and roguish attitudes and remains a threat to U.S. interests and Gulf stability. In this case, regime change in Iraq would not significantly alter future U.S. military requirements from what they are today, and the recommendations for changing our forward presence made elsewhere in this volume would remain valid. In the absence of such upheavals, however, the task at hand is to evaluate future U.S. defense options assuming that the future Gulf security environment remains similar to that of today: intense geopolitical hostility and military rivalry with Iraq and troubled relations with Iran.

In its new defense strategy, the *QDR Report* makes clear that defense of the Persian Gulf will remain a high U.S. strategic priority; no disengagement is contemplated, even if security affairs there heat up and WMD proliferation accelerates. But the *QDR Report* embeds this stance on the Gulf in a larger, pensive vision of where world affairs are headed as globalization accelerates and interacts with new-era geopolitics. It identifies the war on terrorism as one important consideration, but not the only one. In particular, it draws attention to a vast "southern strategic arc of instability," stretching from the Middle East to the Asian littoral, as a new focal point of danger and growing U.S. force operations. While the Persian Gulf is a key part of this southern arc, it is not the only hot region to be considered by a new U.S. defense strategy that increasingly sees the future in global terms rather than as a collection of multiple regions to be considered separately on their own merits.

The *QDR Report* establishes a new sense of defense priorities that differs sharply from the traditional practice of defending the Gulf with a light peacetime presence and initial defense, backed by a big, thunderous reinforcement plan. Instead, this report calls for a stronger forward presence and initial defense that does a better job of deterring on its own, thereby lessening dependence on large, rigidly committed reinforcements so they can be freed for other missions elsewhere. To create the better capabilities that will be needed for this new strategy, the *QDR Report* also calls for U.S. forces in the Gulf and CONUS to be transformed with new information-age technologies and operational concepts for fighting war differently than in the past, especially by using deep-strike airpower in lethal and assertive ways.

Successfully carrying out this agenda in the Gulf promises to be a stiff challenge because local Gulf political currents are flowing in opposite directions. While endangered friends and allies there have reasons to welcome enhanced U.S. security guarantees in principle, they likely will blanch at the idea of a stronger peacetime presence if this means a larger U.S. military footprint on their soil. For them, the idea of high-tech U.S. strike forces from CONUS suddenly descending on them in war and greatly influencing their regional politics in peacetime likely will be controversial for reasons of its own. To a degree, the imperatives of the new U.S. defense strategy and Persian Gulf politics may be at loggerheads in ways that will demand patient reconciliation. Whether this difficult high-wire act can be accomplished is an open question, but it fills the coming era with promise and peril.

Enhanced Forward Deterrence and Defense

In addition to improving defense of the U.S. homeland, the new defense strategy articulated by the *QDR Report* calls for worldwide pursuit of four key strategic goals:

- assuring friends and allies
- dissuading future military competition
- deterring threats and coercion against U.S. interests
- defeating decisively any adversary if deterrence fails.

The goals of assuring, deterring, and defeating have been hardy perennials of U.S. strategy for years. A key issue will be how pursuit of them will be affected if Iraq or Iran acquires nuclear weapons and delivery systems. During the Cold War, the United States relied on its strategic forces to deter nuclear use by adversaries, but the current era is giving rise to a new approach that supplements the threat of second-strike retaliation with defensive systems and counter-WMD conventional strike assets. This change may lead to a requirement to deploy enhanced missile defenses and strike assets in the Gulf in order to assure, deter, and react immediately to nuclear threats. If so, it could create pressures for stationing more U.S. forces, with new capabilities, there in peacetime.

The goal of dissuading future military competition breaks new conceptual ground. Its aim is to use U.S. and allied preparedness efforts to steer potential adversaries away from pursuing competitive military policies that threaten regional stability and common security interests. The idea is that if U.S. and allied forces are strengthened in proper ways, they can deny opponents any hope of gaining military advantages that would enable them to pursue aggressive intentions in peacetime or wartime. Presumably "dissuaded" opponents will conclude that the payoff is not worth the effort, and they therefore will refrain from pursuing destabilizing military buildups, including WMD systems and offensive-oriented conventional forces. In principle, this new goal could bring added pressures for deploying more forces to the Gulf in peacetime, or at least preserving the manpower levels that already exist. These four goals together seemingly create a rationale for a still-sizable U.S. presence there for as long as Iraq and Iran remain geopolitical menaces.

Reinforcing this trend is the *QDR Report* "paradigm shift" in force planning. As part of this shift, the report calls for creation of a stronger overseas presence and forward deterrent postures in critical regions. Accordingly, it directs DOD to maintain "regionally tailored" forces that are forward-stationed in Europe, Northeast Asia, the Asian littoral, the Middle East, and Southwest Asia. The specific aims of such future deployments, it says, are multifold: to enhance deterrence of threats, strengthen alliances and partnerships, maintain favorable regional force balances, and create a broad portfolio of deployed military assets. Importantly, the report also makes clear that stationed U.S. and allied forces should acquire enhanced capabilities to defeat aggression swiftly so that only modest reinforcements are needed, thereby freeing some previously allocated reinforcements for use elsewhere. This judgment applies to Korea, but it also applies to the Gulf, both of which are prime consumers of big reinforcements.

To pursue these aims, the *QDR Report* mandates creation of a "re-oriented U.S. military global posture." It says that the current overseas posture, with its force concentrations in Europe and Northeast Asia, is inadequate in the new strategic environment in which U.S. interests are global and new threats in other areas of the world are emerging. Accordingly, the report calls for new combinations of forward-stationed forces and swiftly available reinforcements. These forces, it says, should pursue new forms of deterrence and defense and extend greater protection to allies and friends in such new areas as missile defenses, information operations, and counterterrorist operations. In addition, it says, the U.S. global military posture should be reoriented to:

- develop a basing system that provides greater flexibility for U.S. forces in critical regions, emphasizing bases and stations beyond Western Europe and Northeast Asia
- provide temporary access to facilities in foreign countries that enable U.S. forces to conduct training and exercises in the absence of permanent ranges and bases
- redistribute forces and equipment based on regional deterrence requirements
- provide enhanced strategic mobility assets for conducting expeditionary operations in distant theaters against enemies armed with WMD systems and other means to deny access to U.S. forces
- employ existing bases and stations, especially in Europe and Northeast Asia, as regional hubs for projecting power elsewhere at long distances.

The *QDR Report* announces a set of specific decisions about changes to U.S. forces stationed in Europe and Asia. For example, it instructs that an Army interim brigade combat team should be deployed to Europe and that in the Western Pacific, DOD should increase CVBG presence and homeport additional surface combatants and submarines. The report announces no specific changes to U.S. forces in the Persian Gulf and nearby regions, but it does put forth strategic guidance on the future. It instructs the Army to explore options for enhancing ground capabilities in the Arabian Gulf, the Navy to develop options to shift some Marine Corps prepositioned equipment from the Mediterranean Sea toward the Arabian Gulf and Indian Ocean, and the Air Force to develop plans to increase contingency basing in the Arabian Gulf and Indian Ocean. While this guidance is general and lacks specificity, its sense of direction is clear: The U.S. military will be aspiring to increase its deterrent and defense capabilities in the Persian Gulf through enhanced forward presence of a new sort. Meanwhile, the Gulf no longer will be viewed as a separate region unto itself but instead as part of a larger geostrategic zone for defense planning that extends into the Arabian Gulf, the Indian Ocean, and Central Asia.

Flexible Wartime Allocations and New Operational Concepts

The changes envisioned by the new defense strategy are not limited to crafting a new global forward presence. Indeed, the strategy's new planning paradigm alters the way in which the entire force posture is sized, allocated in wartime, and programmed. This change, too, has important implications for the Persian Gulf because it goes to the heart of how DOD thinks about its military priorities there.

The *QDR Report* announces a shift from the old "threat-based model" for force planning to a new "capabilities-based model." In the new model, U.S. force planning is intended not to deal with specific threats and contingencies but instead to provide generic capabilities to counter the future capabilities that multiple potential adversaries are likely to field across a wide spectrum of conflicts and new geographical regions. As a result, U.S. forces are to be prepared not only for classic MTWs but also for wars at both the lower and higher ends of the spectrum, including use of WMD systems. Accompanying this focus on generic capabilities is a strong emphasis on making U.S. forces highly flexible and adaptable to deal with ever-shifting challenges ahead. The *QDR Report* offers the judgment that the United States cannot foresee future conflicts and often will be surprised in ways that will compel U.S. forces swiftly to shift strategic gears, deploy to new places, and fight in unexpected ways. Accordingly, it calls for U.S. forces to be modular, scalable, and capable of combining and recombining to form force packages tailored to the mission at hand. As a result, it says, the future force posture should provide a flexible portfolio of assets that can be used in many different ways, rather than in a small set of fixed, predetermined ways.

A key feature of the new paradigm is that U.S. forces are no longer to be optimized for MTWs in Northeast Asia and Southwest Asia. The *QDR Report* instructs that DOD will retain the capacity to wage two MTWs in overlapping time frames there or elsewhere, but preparing for this eventuality will not be the sole preoccupation for planning or interfere with the flexible use of forces in other ways when the situation mandates. In the new paradigm, U.S. forces are to be sized and designed for three purposes:

■ to maintain deterrence and normal military operations in all four major theaters (Europe, Northeast Asia, the East Asian littoral, and the Middle East/Southwest Asia) and conduct small-scale contingencies (SSCs) in them

■ to be able to wage two concurrent MTW conflicts in wartime

■ to assign enough forces for decisive victory in one of these MTW conflicts, including occupation of enemy territory, while in the other war, to rebuff aggression and restore allied borders.

The practical effect of this new paradigm is to create a requirement for three distinct, flexible force packages, as opposed to the two big and inflexible packages of the old era. The first package remains as large as before, with the capability to prosecute a single MTW to complete success. But it is a generic package, capable of being used in multiple places, not just the Persian Gulf or Korea. The second package is also tailored for a generic MTW conflict and high-tech operations, but with fewer forces than the first package—that is, only enough forces to defend successfully, not to counterattack in big ways aimed at occupying enemy territory. The downsizing of forces for this second war, in turn, generates a sizable package of forces that will be available for other missions, including SSCs. Together, these three packages are intended to provide the flexible forces needed both to wage two concurrent MTWs and to carry out a significant number of SSCs, from peacekeeping to small crisis interventions, without worrying that basic U.S. war plans are being shortchanged.

Planning for the Persian Gulf will be affected in concrete ways. In the old era, Gulf defense plans could rely upon the constant commitment of quite large forces for an ambitious war plan, up to one-half of today's posture. In the new era, Gulf plans will have less certainty about firm force commitments because they will need to deal with two distinctly different events: a situation in which equally large forces are made available, and one in which appreciably smaller forces are committed because a big MTW is being waged elsewhere. In the former situation, Gulf plans will continue to contemplate decisive victory, including the destruction of Iraqi forces and occupation of Iraqi territory coupled with imposed regime change. In the latter situation, Gulf plans presumably will be limited to less ambitious goals; for example, the restoration of any allied territory that might be temporarily lost in initial battles, a partial destruction of Iraq forces, and limited incursions onto Iraqi territory.

Accompanying this new paradigm is a far-reaching defense transformation effort that also has important implications for Gulf defense plans because it promises to elevate U.S. warfighting capabilities there. As the *QDR Report* envisions, defense transformation is to be neither a slow

evolutionary crawl into the future nor an impulsive leap-ahead into radically new platforms and weapons brought about by exotic new technologies that will be available only 20 years from now. Instead, transformation
is to be a measured process of change that will unfold purposefully over
many years, gradually altering U.S. forces in growing ways, and steadily el-
evating their capabilities for information-age warfare in the near term,
midterm, and long term. New weapons (such as unmanned aircraft) and
exotic new technologies (hypervelocity missiles) will help propel this
transformation, but modernization with weapons now poised for procurement (such as the F–22 fighter) will play a key role as well. For the
near term and midterm, the *QDR Report* envisions a posture in which
about 10 to 20 percent of combat forces will be fully transformed, and the
remainder will be modernized legacy forces. Many of these fully transformed forces will have spearhead capabilities that enable them to dominate fighting in the early stages, thereby setting the stage for larger modernized legacy forces to win the battle shortly thereafter.

New operational concepts are key to this vision of future warfighting.
In recent years, *Joint Vision 2010* and *Joint Vision 2020* have created a set of
such concepts for guiding force development: full-spectrum dominance,
information operations, dominant maneuver, precision engagement, full-
dimensional protection, and focused logistics. Parallel efforts by the services
have created such additional concepts as network-centric warfare, effects-
based operations, rapid decisive operations, and expeditionary operations.
These developments set the stage for the new operational goals and concepts
adopted by the *QDR Report*.

In addition to better defending the U.S. homeland and space assets,
these new concepts call upon key regional commands to create standing
joint task forces that possess modern command, control, communications, computers, intelligence, surveillance, and reconnaissance (C⁴ISR)
assets and information systems, plus a capacity to take joint operations to
a new level of performance. These new concepts also call for spearhead
forces to be swiftly deployed, in only a few days, to gain early and forcible
entry into crisis zones. They thus reject the notion that stiff antiaccess/area
denial threats will compel American forces to resort to standoff bombard-
ment from long distances outside the crisis zone. Instead, they call upon
forces to gain forcible entry by defeating and overpowering these threats—
a longstanding tenet of U.S. military strategy during the Cold War that
now will be pursued in new, high-tech ways.

Once spearhead forces are deployed and reinforcements begin arriving in the form of modernized legacy forces with new weapons, these operational concepts call for a fast-moving wartime campaign that quickly halts the attack and takes the fight to the enemy through vigorous offensive actions. The core idea is to use information systems, sensors, and munitions to apply joint forces more effectively and efficiently than in the past. The strategic aim is first to fracture the enemy's cohesion and willpower and then to destroy enemy forces through firepower and attrition. Accordingly, U.S. forces are to launch counter-sanctuary strikes deep into enemy territory, destroying WMD assets, industrial facilities, command sites, and logistic networks. These deep strikes are to be carried out by strategic bombers, Air Force and Navy tactical aircraft, and cruise missiles. In addition, air forces are to strike lethally against advancing enemy armored columns, using JSTARS and smart cluster munitions to destroy enemy tanks, infantry fighting vehicles, and artillery before they can advance far into allied territory. Initially, this air effort is to be accompanied by ground operations aimed at blocking the enemy advance. But as soon as possible, the rapid buildup of ground forces is designed to permit a quick transition to the offensive in the form of rapid engagements, fast maneuvers, and lethal firepower aimed at crushing remaining enemy forces. As this offensive unfolds, U.S. forces are to restore allied borders and then advance into enemy territory in a manner dictated by political goals at the time.

At first glance, this campaign seems like an updated version of Operation *Desert Storm*, but it differs in important respects because of its emphasis on information systems and new high-tech weaponry. If carried out effectively, it will unfold faster than in the past because U.S. forces will deploy more rapidly and operate at a higher tempo. It will embody joint operations—the careful integration of air, naval, and ground forces—to a greater degree. It will conduct these joint operations in parallel fashion rather than sequentially as in the past. It will make greater use of space assets for communications, intelligence, and battlefield coordination. It will strive to network naval operations by blending the offensive and defensive actions of multiple types of ships and other assets. It will make even greater use of airpower and smart munitions, along with unmanned aircraft, relying on their growing capacity to destroy targets with great accuracy and precision. It will employ ground forces in new and different ways as well, dispersing them across the battlefield, advancing at rapid rates, and employing armor, artillery, attack helicopters, and missiles to tear apart enemy formations.

Allied Transformation

As U.S. forces transform to pursue these new operational concepts, parallel progress by allied forces can further enhance prospects for combined operations. Conversely, if these allies fail to upgrade their forces, the effect will be to place even larger burdens on U.S. forces. The GCC countries are unlikely to enlarge their forces further in a wholesale way or to pursue transformation as robustly as the United States is doing. But taking into account their political willpower and fiscal realities, modest improvements may be possible.

Better configuring their forces to ward off the initial stages of an Iraqi surprise coup de main strike rather than to sustain a long attrition battle with Iraq might make a big contribution not only to allied security but to the U.S. rapid reinforcement strategy as well. If allies can be motivated to pursue enhanced multinational collaboration and coalition operations (a big if), this step offers an excellent and inexpensive way to upgrade their defense capacities. Joint and combined operations skills are another critical area in which improvements could make a huge impact. Acquiring new information systems, sensors, and smart munitions could strengthen already-modern allied air forces for ground attack roles, thereby reducing the vulnerability of their outgunned ground forces. Improving their forces across the board with other new weapons and enhanced training would make them more interoperable with transforming U.S. forces that will be acquiring new technologies and operational doctrines. But an even better idea might be to focus allied programs on areas in which their forces are especially vulnerable or on niche capabilities that they could use to help defeat antiaccess/area denial threats in ways that facilitate the swift arrival and entry of U.S. forces. High-leverage improvements in these areas might help transform a still-dangerous Gulf force balance into greater security and stability.

As chapter four underscored, the ability of the Gulf states to significantly improve their military capabilities is open to doubt. But even if allied forces improve in these ways, U.S. forces will remain primarily responsible for defending the Gulf against major threats. However, new operational concepts create a vision of a new type of warfare that has major implications for how another Persian Gulf war could be fought. In essence, a future war will be waged faster, more boldly, and more lethally than in the past. Whether these operational concepts will be brought fully to life will depend upon the success of the U.S. military transformation effort. Much also will depend upon preparations made in the Persian Gulf for supporting these operations, enemy efforts to foil them through improved forces and asymmetric strategies, and the normal frictions of war. But to the extent this new vision comes into existence, it promises to widen further the superiority gap of U.S. forces over opponents there. It will increase the premium on forces stationed in the Gulf and on early reinforcements, but it may decrease requirements for total reinforcements.

These changes could also alter political perceptions of U.S. forces and operations in the Gulf. The transformed U.S. military could come to be seen as an even stronger source of assurance and security among friends and allies and as a formidable barrier to aggression by opponents. Yet it also will be seen as a high-tech leviathan, thereby reinforcing the controversial image of the United States as a superpower capable of casting aside the controls and restraints normally placed on nations. How countries in the Gulf and elsewhere will react to these signals and images is uncertain. But one thing seems clear: U.S. diplomats may see their influence and respect grow, but they will have a sales job to perform. So will U.S. foreign policy as a whole.

Future U.S. Force Options

During the past year alone, the global war on terrorism and the "axis of evil" concept have buffeted how the United States views its strategic priorities in the Persian Gulf and how countries there view the U.S. forces assigned to their region. What the future will produce is uncertain, but a few things seem clear. Unless the mounting geopolitical strains in the Gulf are resolved, the United States will be compelled to continue preparing sizable forces for missions there and in nearby regions. Yet the size and internal configuration of the posture allocated for these missions a decade from now likely will differ considerably from that of today. This likely will be the case for both the peacetime presence and wartime reinforcements. The proper response to the coming era of change is to guide this change in constructive directions, rather than drift with the times in a manner that allows events to take their own course.

Today's force posture for the Persian Gulf is caught between crosscurrents pulling in opposite directions. This clearly is the case for the peacetime presence. Whereas requirements may increase as WMD proliferation accelerates, friendly Gulf countries will still want U.S. security guarantees. Owing to domestic political pressures, however, they will not want to see the U.S. footprint on their soil increase, and some will want it to decrease. Crosscurrents also apply to U.S. wartime reinforcement plans. Future requirements will mandate that transformed American forces remain capable of swiftly deploying to the Gulf in order to win any war there. Yet U.S. global defense strategy is mandating greater flexibility in ways that could result in fewer reinforcements being automatically available for Gulf missions.

How can these crosscurrents best be handled? What *should* be avoided is a flawed process that either impulsively bows to the prevailing political winds in strategically erroneous ways or mechanically decreases or increases force commitments according to some arbitrary formula anchored in manpower or other simplistic measures of merit. Above all, sound planning and wise decisions are needed. Crosscurrents are nothing new. They have been affecting U.S. defense planning in the Gulf and other regions for the past 50 years. In the past, the United States has reacted best to them when it strove to create a force posture that was militarily effective, financially affordable, and politically palatable. On many occasions it succeeded by paying close attention to the details of designing forces for missions in ways aimed at harmonizing its goals and striking a sensible balance among competing priorities. The same approach is needed again.

A future of change thus can best be handled by redesigning U.S. forces for the Persian Gulf so that they will be able to perform the new missions ahead in acceptable ways. The main goal should be to create a new peacetime presence and wartime reinforcement plan that interlock to carry out U.S. defense strategy, but do not establish an overbearing political footprint in the Gulf nor drain the overall posture of too many forces and resources. At the moment, it would be premature to write a fixed blueprint for the future in either area. Indeed, the future Gulf posture may be constantly evolving and changing. But it is not too early to think deeply about the future and its possibilities. An analytical process aimed at surveying the options ahead along with their tradeoffs may help illuminate future choices and establish a sense of direction for the near term and beyond.

This analytical process will need to take into account the full range of considerations affecting U.S. force preparations for the Gulf. DOD is quite skilled at assessing force requirements and priorities for warfighting. But even for the U.S. Government as a whole, assessing how military forces contribute to the pursuit of larger political and strategic goals is more difficult. The many sensitivities and complex nuances of the Gulf region will need to be addressed in the future. How many forces, with what kinds of capabilities, are needed to underwrite U.S. foreign policy and diplomacy there? How many forces are too many, unproductive at the margins, or counterproductive? How can the force presence best be combined with other regional policies, including security assistance and multilateral cooperation with allies, to achieve national objectives? These issues are hard to analyze, but they will need cogent answers if the future U.S. military presence is to be well constructed. So far, DOD has relied on its theater engagement plans (TEPs) to address these issues, but the methodology employed for the TEP process falls short of what is needed to analyze the relationship between military means and political ends. DOD and the interagency community need something better if future options are to be analyzed thoroughly and acted upon wisely.

An Evolving Peacetime Presence

The need to think in dynamic rather than static terms especially applies to the U.S. peacetime presence in the Persian Gulf, which may change often during the coming decade and beyond. Perhaps the most important consideration is that owing to the war on terrorism and other geostrategic priorities, CENTCOM may be required to carry out significant military operations across its entire area of responsibility (AOR), which stretches from the Horn of Africa to Central Asia and the Indian Ocean. Events in and around Afghanistan, coupled with growing military assistance to such countries as Yemen to combat terrorism, mean that the Persian Gulf may no longer be the sole focus of significant U.S. force operations by CENTCOM and other commands with growing responsibilities along the endangered southern arc.

Unless Iraq and Iran move away (under their own volition or by events) from being perpetual adversaries, U.S. requirements for peacetime presence in the Persian Gulf seem likely to increase or at least remain stable. If Iraq and Iran acquire WMD and delivery systems, this development will underscore the need for sizable U.S. forces to stay continuously in the region for assurance and deterrence purposes. In addition, the United States may need to station some forces that deal expressly with the WMD threat—for example, additional Patriot (PAC–3) batteries for missile defense and high-tech aircraft for launching strikes against WMD targets on short notice. Improvements to Iraqi conventional forces in ways that enhance the risk of a surprise attack could have a similar effect. For as long as this threat remains real, U.S. military planners are likely to want to station an Air Force fighter wing, a CVBG and ARG, and Army prepositioned equipment sets for three brigades there.

A key task will be determining how the *QDR Report* guidance for enhancing the capacity swiftly to project more Army, Air Force, and Marine combat forces into the Gulf is to be carried out. Increased strategic airlift is one potential answer, but it is not a stand-alone solution. Today's U.S. military and civil reserve air fleet airlift force can carry only about 25,000 tons per day to the Gulf. A feasible increase of 2,500 to 5,000 tons daily would make only a small dent in the extra 100,000 to 150,000 tons that must be lifted. Additional sealift from CONUS can help, but taking into account the dynamics of loading, sailing, and unloading, even fast cargo ships require a month or more to supply the Gulf. Political sensitivities likely rule out any wholesale increase of shore basing for more equipment. These realities suggest that the only viable course is increased sea-based prepositioning of Army and Marine equipment near the Gulf, coupled with low-profile improvements to allied airbases so that they absorb U.S. air reinforcements in the Gulf and elsewhere. This option would not be cheap, but it could enhance the capacity of U.S. ground and air forces to deploy not only to the Gulf but also to other regions, including South Asia and the Indian Ocean.

Creating spearhead forces for early and forcible entry means that preparatory measures will be needed in the Gulf to receive them. U.S. combat forces remaining in the Gulf must be designed to be a leading edge of the spearhead forces and thus may be early recipients of new technologies and weapons as well as additional prepositioned equipment and war reserve stocks of smart munitions. Measures also may be needed to reduce the vulnerability of local bases and infrastructure to enemy missile strikes and other antiaccess/area denial threats. For example, steps to harden command posts, airfields, and seaports further will likely make sense. Such steps may not increase the number of troops and combat units that are deployed, but they would result in increased DOD spending on the Gulf and in a higher profile for U.S. forces.

This upward trend in requirements does not mean that efforts to reduce the current U.S. military footprint in the Gulf, or at least minimize its future growth, are doomed. If a spearhead posture is created that better enables high-priority U.S. forces in CONUS to deploy more rapidly than now, this development will help alleviate any pressures to station significantly bigger combat forces in the Gulf if threats of surprise attack grow. Much also will depend upon Operation *Southern Watch*. If it is discontinued, or if its daily requirement for air sorties declines, the United States may no longer need a full Air Force fighter wing and a Navy CVBG in the Gulf full time. Perhaps the Air Force wing could be reduced to one or two squadrons or rely more heavily on unmanned aircraft. Or perhaps Navy carriers and amphibious ships will no longer need to patrol the northern waters of the Gulf as often as now. Such developments could help visibly reduce the U.S. presence.

Other footprint-reducing measures are possible. Better information systems may allow the U.S. military to reduce reliance on forward-stationed command staffs as well as intelligence and communications facilities. The U.S. military will continue to need access to Saudi Arabia and its airspace, but if that country objects to the U.S. presence on its soil, headquarters assets and Air Force combat aircraft can be redeployed to Qatar or Kuwait, and the Navy can increase reliance on ports in the United Arab Emirates and Kuwait. As discussed in chapter two, initial steps in this direction already are under way in Qatar. More steps may be necessary in the future, depending upon U.S. needs for additional infrastructure and the attitudes of host governments. If necessary, another response is to rely increasingly on temporary rotational assignments of U.S. combat forces rather than near-permanent stationing of units there. Similarly, some U.S. equipment sets and war reserve stocks can be moved offshore to cargo ships or mobile sea platforms. Few of these measures may be optimal or cost-effective, but they provide viable alternatives for making the best of a difficult situation if the Gulf political atmosphere mandates a lower U.S. profile.

Three options help frame the directions that the peacetime presence could take over the next decade and beyond:

The first option is a presence of the routine manpower level or slightly higher, but with a different mix of units and significantly greater capabilities as a result of transformation and modernization. For example, the posture might have fewer fighter aircraft but a command center with better information systems, more Patriot air defense missiles, additional prepositioned stocks, a fighter wing composed of F–22s and Joint Strike Fighters, and a Navy carrier flying F/A–18 E/Fs.

The second option is a presence with significantly less ashore manpower that might come about if Gulf political conditions mandate a big reduction in the U.S. footprint. In the extreme case, ashore forces might be reduced to token levels (for example, 1,000 personnel for security assistance and other consultative functions). The total U.S. posture in the Gulf thus would fall to 10,000 to 15,000 troops. This development would compel American strategy to rely on sea-based forces, long-distance oversight with space systems and other virtual presence assets, and ultrafast wartime reinforcement for initial defense. Alternatively, this second option might allow for 5,000 personnel ashore, thus permitting a total Gulf presence of 15,000 to 20,000 troops. The ashore posture presumably would entail a command staff and fewer combat aircraft than now.

The third option envisions a bigger posture that might be needed if security conditions worsen. For example, a posture that includes an additional fighter wing, an Army brigade, and 2 Patriot battalions would elevate the routine presence to 43,000 to 48,000 troops.

Whether these or other options are used to redesign peacetime presence remains to be seen. Regardless, the manpower level is not the key issue. What matters is whether the future U.S. presence effectively meets military requirements in ways that are politically palatable. The size of the posture matters, but its internal configuration and capabilities matter a good deal more. A bigger posture that is poorly designed may not perform as well, in military and strategic terms, than a well-designed smaller posture. Conversely, a bigger posture that is well designed and performs effectively but unobtrusively may elicit fewer footprint complaints than a smaller posture that is both ineffective and obtrusive. These tradeoffs are worth taking into account as options for the future peacetime presence are weighed.

Options for Wartime Reinforcement

Clearly, a single plan for wartime reinforcement of the Persian Gulf will not suffice for the coming years. To provide the enhanced global flexibility demanded by the new U.S. defense strategy while still defending the Gulf in effective ways, DOD will need to design a spectrum of reinforcement options. Such options always have existed in theory. But firmly installing them in the DOD planning process—to the point where they are reflected in Secretary of Defense guidance, service programs, DOD budgets, and the operational plans of combatant commands—is another matter. Carrying out this task so that the necessary flexible capabilities are actually created, not merely endorsed rhetorically, frames the agenda ahead.

Four illustrative options are put forth here for both the early arriving forces and the additional reinforcements that might be deployed as a function of the war and its requirements:

The first option is to create the spearhead force envisioned in the new strategy. This force could be employed by itself for small crises or serve as the vanguard of larger, later-arriving reinforcements for bigger wars. Such a high-tech force presumably would be composed of about three or four Air Force fighter wings, one CVBG and one ARG, plus four to six Army and Marine brigades under command of a standing joint task force equipped with the necessary C^{4}ISR architecture for highly integrated joint operations. Some of these forces can be provided by units stationed in the Gulf, but the remainder will need to come from elsewhere, including CONUS. These forces will need to be capable of deploying within a few days, forcibly entering in the face of antiaccess/area denial threats, suppressing WMD threats, and vigorously opposing an enemy advance so that later-arriving reinforcements can appear and ultimately win the war. These forces will need to be fully transformed with modernized weapons and new technologies, they will need a support infrastructure in the Gulf, and they will need to be interlocked with U.S. and allied initial defense plans there.

The second option is a medium-sized strike package that would permit U.S. forces to halt an enemy invasion and restore allied borders but not occupy the enemy country. Counting the spearhead force, this posture would total about five to six Air Force fighter wings, three to four Army and Marine divisions, and two CVBGs. Taking into account the growing lethality and survivability of U.S. forces, a posture this size seems capable of accomplishing its limited goals.

The third option is a full-sized MTW posture that would permit decisive victory and occupation of enemy territory. It would include about 10 fighter wings, 6 to 7 divisions, and 4 CVBGs.

The fourth option provides the additional forces if a larger regional war must be waged, perhaps against both Iraq and Iran. Illustratively, it totals 15 fighter wings, 10 divisions, and 6 CVBGs. Together these four options offer a range of alternative manpower commitments: about 125,000 troops for the spearhead posture; 225,000 for the medium-sized strike package; 425,000 for the full-sized MTW posture; and over 600,000 for the biggest posture.

Normally, CENTCOM would have the first two postures—the spearhead force backed by enough additional assets to create the medium-sized strike package—at its ready disposal. Forces for the other two bigger options would be assigned when conditions warrant. Whereas only one of the peacetime presence options can be pursued at any single time, the United States could fund all four reinforcement options at the same time and, when a crisis arises, select the best option for the situation at hand. Alternatively, it could use these options as an escalation ladder that could be climbed one rung at a time, starting with the spearhead force and culminating with whichever larger posture could get the job done. Thus, these four reinforcement options would greatly expand the range of choices open to the U.S. Government in a crisis—a good thing for a region whose complexities defy single-point solutions and perpetually mandate as much flexibility as possible.

Taking Stock of the Options

While the United States has multiple options at its disposal, the new defense strategy seems headed to a new force posture for the Persian Gulf. This posture is anchored in a new peacetime presence that has greater forward defense capabilities than now but little, if any, additional manpower. Supporting this new presence will be a newly flexible reinforcement plan that may allocate fewer forces than before, but these forces will have enhanced combat capabilities through faster deployment rates and transformed weapons and doctrines. If this new strategy and force posture is implemented, will it be militarily effective in ways that allow the United States to win any future Gulf war? The answer is yes, but only if the United States continues to take new-era Gulf defense affairs seriously rather than assume continued predominance simply because its forces are the best in the world.

Even the world's best forces can be unhinged if they are unprepared for the specific wars that they will be fighting. Key to the new defense strategy for the Gulf is the spearhead force, for it permits continued reliance on a small peacetime presence coupled with a reduced reinforcement plan. If it succeeds, it should be able to work with allied forces to contain an enemy attack in the forward areas, thereby permitting a medium-sized package of later-arriving U.S. reinforcements to restore borders and badly batter the enemy. But its success should not be taken for granted. Not only must its reinforcing units be able to deploy swiftly, but also its entire posture must be able rapidly to overcome future antiaccess/area denial threats. Success at this endeavor is feasible but could be endangered if unhardened airbases, unprotected ports, and warships steaming in the narrow confines of the Gulf are vulnerable to enemy missile attacks. Concrete measures to reduce these vulnerabilities are imperative.

Nor should the United States assume that its powerful air forces and cruise missiles are a stand-alone solution to winning future Gulf wars. U.S. bombers and tactical combat aircraft can inflict great damage on enemy forces, but only if they remain capable of surviving enemy air defenses that may improve in the future, and only if they have enough sensors and smart munitions (such as joint direct attack munitions, joint standoff weapons, and Skeets) to perform their missions fully. Cruise missiles can help for attacking fixed targets, but they are costly silver bullets, and enough of them must be available to meet requirements. Moreover, even fully prepared air forces cannot be relied upon to defeat a large enemy armored force on their own. True, their sensors and smart munitions give air forces a theoretical capacity to destroy a great deal of enemy armor if they have enough time to carry out their mission in a permissive environment. But the environment might not be fully permissive, and in any event, an Iraqi ground attack might be able to seize a big chunk of Kuwait or beyond before a mounting U.S. air campaign stops it in its tracks. To stiffen the forward defense and to conduct later counterattacks, significant U.S. ground forces will be needed. Moreover, these ground forces will need to provide more than spotters for air attacks and light mechanized assets; they will need enough armor and artillery to wage a serious ground war of maneuver and shock action. In all of these areas of preparedness for air, ground, and naval forces, DOD will need to remain attentive to future requirements and transformation priorities, while also being cognizant of Gulf political realities and pursuing the art of the possible there.

If this portrayal helps identify the long-term Gulf defense agenda ahead, how should the United States act in the near future? The bottom line is that, provided the Persian Gulf does not head toward war in the coming period, this is not the time for major, abrupt changes in the U.S. defense posture for handling Gulf security affairs. That is, this is not the time for reducing the routine peacetime presence there in big ways even if political pressures for a smaller footprint intensify. Emerging military requirements are pulling in the opposite direction, and cuts in U.S. troops might be misread by adversaries as suggesting a weakening of U.S. resolve, thereby undermining deterrence. Nor is this the time for a big increase in the normal peacetime presence; it is not needed now and might not be needed in the future, and it would exacerbate the footprint controversy.

A "steady at the helm" approach, however, does not mean that the United States should stand pat in the Gulf because, over the long haul, significant change is both inevitable and desirable. Even if manpower levels and combat formations remain constant, the coming introduction of new weapons and systems will elevate American combat capabilities and alter the manner in which they operate. Similar to U.S. military transformation as a whole, these and other changes should start in the near term and then accelerate later as part of a long-term plan for achieving a coherent goal.

For the immediate future, DOD should add new capabilities as the opportunity presents itself and remove others if they are no longer needed or are too controversial to keep there. Meanwhile, it can start creating the spearhead posture for the Gulf, an effort that will affect both the peacetime presence and wartime reinforcement posture in important ways. It can also set about to create the new operational plan and associated programs needed to breathe life into its new medium-sized reinforcement package. If DOD can accomplish these important measures over the next few years, it will be off to a good start in becoming well prepared to handle Gulf security affairs over the long haul.

Conceivably, if Iraq and Iran are removed from the strategic chess-board as rogue powers, the Gulf would become more stable, and U.S. military requirements would diminish, perhaps substantially. But assuming one or both of these countries remain hostile amid a setting of geopolitical strain along the southern arc, the United States would need to continue carrying weighty Gulf responsibilities yet would be acting differently than in the past. Since 1991, U.S. strategy has relied on a small peacetime presence and a vulnerable initial defense backed by a big reinforcement plan in wartime. By contrast, the new U.S. defense strategy aspires to reverse this equation by creating a stronger forward defense so that some reinforcements can be freed for other purposes. While this strategy is a global construct, it may have an especially big impact on Gulf defense plans.

To carry out the new strategy there, this analysis argues, the task of shaping the future peacetime U.S. military presence is not to decrease or increase it in some mechanical way, but instead to redesign it—with transformed capabilities to perform the new missions ahead—in ways that are militarily effective and politically palatable. The same theme of redesigning, rather than arbitrarily increasing or decreasing, applies to the wartime U.S. commitment. Owing to growing requirements else-where, the days are ending in which nearly one-half of the U.S. military posture can be rigidly allocated to Gulf missions and focused solely on an old-style war against Iraq. To realize the vision of the *QDR Report,* a more flexible approach will be needed, one that provides a broader geostrategic focus and a wider spectrum of options ranging from forces smaller than now to those that are as large (or even larger) but prepared to fight differently than before. Reinforcements for Gulf missions also will need to be transformed with new capabilities for new operational concepts. Creation of small, high-tech spearhead forces for early entry could strengthen U.S. forward defenses while offsetting the need for both a larger peacetime presence and a big, inflexible reinforcement plan.

Chapter Six

The Role of Outside Powers

Richard D. Sokolsky and Eugene B. Rumer

A fter the collapse of the Soviet Union and America's stunning success in the Gulf War, the United States stood virtually unopposed in the Persian Gulf region. Over the coming decade, however, the United States is likely to find itself on a more crowded playing field as several outside powers, notably European countries, Russia, and China, compete for enhanced influence and access. These countries, driven by geopolitical, economic, and strategic motivations, will pursue their own agendas, objectives, and priorities that will often clash as well as converge with U.S. policies and interests. Their support or opposition will be an important determinant of U.S. success in implementing its policy initiatives.

This chapter provides an overview of the objectives, interests, and policies of these external actors and the challenges and opportunities that they present for U.S. regional security strategy.[1] It will focus on the stance of these countries toward U.S. military operations in the Persian Gulf and actions they might take that could upset the geopolitical status quo or balance of military forces in the region.

The Europeans

The United States and Europe share a number of common goals and interests in the Gulf. These include securing access to Persian Gulf oil supplies at reasonable prices; preventing the spread of terrorism and weapons of mass destruction (WMD); and fostering peace, stability, and prosperity. Nonetheless, over the years some of the most acute tensions in the transatlantic relationship have stemmed from U.S. and European disagreements in the Persian Gulf, especially over the most effective policies to achieve these goals. The most contentious disputes have revolved around the American use of military force and the imposition of sanctions to moderate the behavior of Iraq and Iran. These differences are likely to persist, given the high stakes involved and the political, diplomatic, and economic investments of both the United States and Europe in the region. However, a key question for the future of the transatlantic relationship and U.S.-European security cooperation in the Gulf is the extent to which the events of September 11, 2001, have transformed European attitudes toward the application of Western military power in the region in pursuit of common interests.

European Interests

Europe has extensive strategic, political, economic, and historical/cultural interests in the Persian Gulf.[2] As noted in chapter two, Europe depends heavily on oil imports from the Gulf, notwithstanding its efforts to diversify sources of energy supplies from North Africa, Russia, and the Atlantic Basin. Indeed, most of Iran's oil and gas exports are consumed by the European market, and the same will be true for Iraqi energy exports once it is able to shed sanctions that have prevented the reconstruction of its heavily damaged oil infrastructure. Moreover, European dependence on Gulf energy supplies is likely to grow substantially over the next 10 to 15 years, particularly as North Sea oil and gas resources are depleted.

Closely related to European energy imports from the Gulf is two-way trade between the regions. Presently, neither Iraq nor Iran is a lucrative market for European goods, services, and capital. Also, the European Union (EU) initiative to cultivate stronger economic relations with the Gulf Cooperation Council (GCC) states has yet to yield substantial dividends. Nonetheless, several European countries, notably the United Kingdom, France, and Germany, are captivated by the long-term market potential of Iraq and Iran. Some of the Continent's largest companies, such as the giant French energy firm TotalFinaElf, hope to cash in on the economic reconstruction needs of Iraq and Iran, which some estimates put at well over $300 billion. TotalFinaElf, for example, has already reportedly signed contracts with the Iraqi government to develop some of Iraq's largest oil fields once sanctions have been lifted. It has already made a substantial investment in the exploration and development of Iran's largest offshore deposits of oil and gas as well.

The growing presence of Muslims/Arabs in European countries is another factor that influences European attitudes and policies in the Persian Gulf region. Over the past 2 decades, a substantial influx of immigrants from the Muslim/Arab world has occurred into Europe, notably France, Germany, Spain, Italy, and Belgium. Moreover, the population growth among these groups is higher than that of native populations, and Muslim/Arab immigrants and citizens, both legal and illegal, have limited economic and educational opportunities and experience a host of related economic and political woes. They also maintain close ties with religious and ethnic brethren in their countries of origin. Because of their relatively poor political, economic, and social conditions, the dissatisfied and disenchanted Arab/Muslim populations of Europe provide a potential source of terrorism and Islamic extremism. As a consequence, many European governments and the EU more broadly are extremely sensitive to U.S. and Western policies in the Arab/Islamic world that might inflame the anger of Muslims throughout Europe.

Security Perspectives and the Use of Force

In the past decade, American and European differences in the Gulf have been most evident over the question of sanctions and U.S. efforts to obtain European support for the use of American military force in the region. Since *Desert Storm* in 1991, only the United Kingdom has consistently supported U.S. military action against Iraq. During this period, Britain's European allies (and, on occasion, the United Kingdom itself) have sought to constrain American dominance in the region and beyond,[3] to promote the European policy of "critical dialogue" and engagement with Iran, to ease U.S. and international sanctions on both Iraq and Iran, and to undermine the American policy of dual containment. Several factors and attitudes have shaped and will continue to influence these European perspectives.

First, most European governments do not feel as threatened by Iraq and Iran as does the United States. For both historical and cultural reasons, moreover, those European countries that are concerned about Iraqi and Iranian WMD capabilities are prepared to tolerate a higher degree of vulnerability than the United States.

Second, even those European countries that worry about Iraq and Iran prefer to rely primarily on deterrence and non-military means, such as dialogue, trade, and engagement, to combat the NBC threat and to moderate extremist behavior more generally. Indeed, most European countries reject the very notions of rogue states and the axis of evil, not only because they challenge the European commitment to engagement but also because they create a moral clarity that most find crude and simplistic. The fact that the European nonconfrontational approach to Iraq and Iran has yielded virtually no results has not dissuaded the Europeans from their course.

Third, European governments generally do not see threats in the Gulf in military terms. They fear, in the words of EU Minister of External Affairs Christopher Patten, that the United States believes that the projection of military power is the only basis of true security.[4] Most believe that internal instability rather than external aggression poses the greatest challenge to the security of the Gulf states. Similarly, they believe that military power is insufficient to tackle the threat of terrorism in the Gulf and that the root causes of terrorism can only be eradicated by a combination of foreign aid and development and humanitarian assistance—what is known in EU parlance as soft power.[5]

Finally, on a more philosophical level, reflecting Europe's tragic historical experience with the unrestrained use of military power and its experience in building the institutions of the European Union, most European governments prefer to see global threats handled multilaterally or by international organizations on the basis of the rule of law and established international norms.[6] European inability to project force independently on a global scale reinforces this orientation.

These general European attitudes toward the use of force are deep-seated. Most Europeans, because of historical experience, also are skeptical of the notions that Western-style democracy could be imposed on Iraq from the outside and that the creation of democracy there would unleash a tidal wave of democratization throughout the Arab world.[7] It would be a mistake, therefore, to underestimate their influence on how European countries would react to future U.S. military actions against Iraq (or Iran). While these views help explain both why many European leaders have decried the "unilateralist urge" in Washington as "profoundly misguided"[8] and why many have reservations about a preventive U.S. military attack on Iraq, these predilections should not necessarily be seen as a bellwether of how European countries would respond to a U.S. decision to use military force to overthrow Saddam.

The Impact of September 11

The debate in the United States over whether to use military force to remove Saddam Husayn from power has thrust European views on the use of force in the Persian Gulf to the forefront of transatlantic relations. Many, though by no means all, European governments remain uneasy about unilateral, preemptive U.S. military action against Iraq. European angst reflects not only concern that forcible efforts at regime change could plunge Iraq into chaos, destabilize the broader region, and distract from the war on terrorism, but also a deeper skepticism about U.S. foreign policy in general. Perhaps more importantly, European governments understand the dilemma they would face if the United States decided to use force to oust Saddam: if they support the United States, they risk alienating much of the

Arab-Islamic world and their own publics. But if they remain neutral or oppose U.S. military operations, they could damage transatlantic relations.

Since September 11, moreover, European misgivings about American unilateralism and the U.S. axis of evil rhetoric have been tempered by the growing recognition that Europeans cannot expect to have political influence in Washington if they have no effective military power to contribute to the war on terrorism—or, as put by NATO Secretary-General Lord Robertson, European governments will lose all credibility if they continue to carp from the sidelines rather than develop the capabilities they need to work in partnership with the United States in defense of common interests.[9] Equally important, European countries understand that transatlantic solidarity could suffer a serious blow if the U.S. Armed Forces continue to bear most of the costs of the war on terrorism while Europe takes a pass. They also understand that withholding political solidarity and military assistance in a future Iraqi contingency could seal the fate of NATO as a serious military alliance, even if it continues to have a future as a political organization.

Because of the stark realities created by September 11, it is possible that, as in the case of Afghanistan, some European countries—particularly the United Kingdom and perhaps Spain, Italy, and several new NATO members—would offer military forces to support a U.S. military campaign against Iraq, even if Iraq is not linked to the attacks of September 11 or to other terrorist operations by al Qaeda. Turkey appears more receptive to supporting U.S. ambitions regarding Iraq. Turkey's new government, led by a moderate Islamic party, is nervous over the prospects of an American military attack on Iraq, given the impact it could have on the longstanding Kurdish problem and on the Turkish economy, as well as overwhelming public opposition to an American war on Iraq. However, the Turkish government attaches great value to its relationship with the United States, and its long-term economic interests would be better served if Saddam's removal led to a lifting of sanctions on Iraq. Consequently, Ankara might be more favorably disposed to allow use of Turkish territory to support U.S. military operations if Washington addressed its economic and security concerns. Most notably, these include assurances that an independent state of Kurdistan would not be created and that the United States will provide financial and military assistance to compensate Turkey for any losses it incurs from the military operation and its aftermath.[10]

Moreover, an even greater number of European countries might offer military assistance and strong diplomatic support under two conditions:

■ If there were clear and unambiguous evidence that Iraq was in material breach of United Nations Security Council (UNSC) resolution 1441 and the Security Council had authorized U.S. military action against Iraq. Even in the absence of such approval, however, the United States is likely to succeed in garnering broad European support for a U.S. invasion of Iraq if it is seen as having made a genuine diplomatic effort to gain UN backing for its actions and Iraq had failed to avail itself of every opportunity to avert a military confrontation. In other words, European countries will be more likely to bandwagon with the United States to the extent that the Bush administration follows a multilateral approach and its decision to use force to disarm Iraq commands broad international legitimacy and support.

■ If the United States succeeds in convincing its European allies that it has a coherent plan for the creation of a stable postwar order in Iraq and the region writ large. For Europeans, the depth of the U.S. commitment to regime change will be measured by whether this plan envisions a substantial and sustained commitment of U.S. forces in post-Saddam Iraq and an equally robust U.S. political and economic commitment to postwar nation-building and reconstruction. Conveying this sense of resolve and purpose, moreover, will make it easier for European governments to gain domestic political and public support for the deployment of European forces for both military and post-conflict stability operations—a role that many European governments will want to play to protect their own equities in postwar Iraq.[11]

In sum, it will be difficult for many European governments to resist strong U.S. leadership for a multilateral approach to disarming Iraq. Indeed, as one prominent expert has noted, European governments understand the extremely negative political and strategic consequences that would result from a U.S. decision to use military force unilaterally or within the framework of a narrowly backed U.S.-led coalition. If this were to happen due to the absence of European support, transatlantic relations would be seriously damaged, the authority and credibility of the UNSC would be tarnished (perhaps irreparably), Europe and NATO would be further marginalized in U.S. security calculations, and Europe's common foreign and security policy (CFSP) would be in tatters.[12]

Whether the United States would accept European offers of military forces in an operation against Iraq, and what type of contribution these assets would make to the campaign, are separate questions that are beyond the scope of this chapter.

Russia

The breakup of the Soviet Union brought about a major shift in Moscow's policy in the Middle East in general and Persian Gulf in particular. Prior to 1991, Moscow's policy in the Middle East was to a very large degree a subset of its global confrontation with the United States. Following the Soviet collapse in 1991, Moscow's policy has been a product of its chaotic domestic political and policymaking environment dominated by special interests and lacking a set of firm political, ideological, or bureaucratic rules to adjudicate among them. The result has been a set of mutually contradictory policies pursued simultaneously by various arms and branches of the Russian government and corporate entities.[13]

The events of September 11 and the decision by the Russian government to support the United States in its war on terrorism are not likely to have a significant impact on Russian policy in this area, as it remains heavily dependent on powerful domestic interests. Russia's residual domestic weakness will serve as an effective constraint on its government's ability to organize and mobilize its limited national resources on behalf of a coherent, consistent, and sustainable policy with well-defined aims. Rather, Russian policy in the Gulf is more likely to cater to the diverse domestic interests pushing it in different directions. Ironically, Russian participation in the U.S.-led antiterrorist coalition may further sharpen the internal contradictions in Russian policy.

Russian Interests in the Gulf

The Gulf's place on Russia's foreign policy agenda is determined to a large extent by the influence of two major domestic lobbies: energy and arms. As the world's premier oil-producing region and home to a uniquely well-funded arms bazaar, the Persian Gulf is enormously important to Russian oil producers and weapons manufacturers. For the former, as well as for Russia's national treasury (given the prominent place of energy exports in the country's foreign trade and economy in general), what happens in the Gulf and how it affects the price of oil can mean the difference between economic survival and collapse. For Russia's defense industrial complex, the cash-rich Gulf states are among the most prized customers, as domestic procurement orders have largely dried up as a result of Russian economic crises of the 1990s. Export markets became a way—for some the only way—to survive for the once-mighty Russian defense sector.[14]

Russia's Atomic Energy Ministry (MINATOM) has also at times exerted a strong influence over Russian policy in the Gulf. MINATOM, in particular, has played a key role in shaping and sustaining Moscow's relationship with Tehran through its pursuit of the Bushehr nuclear power plant project and other nuclear power reactors under development. Indeed, it would be difficult to name another corporate or bureaucratic player in the contemporary Russian political landscape whose influence on foreign and national security policy rivals that of MINATOM.[15]

Although diminished in stature and political influence since 1991, the professional national security bureaucracy remains an important source of influence in Russian foreign policy if only by virtue of its formal stewardship of the process. Rooted in and nostalgic for its privileged and powerful Soviet past, this group has yet to find its new bearings in post-Soviet Russia and in its outlook harbors a good deal of inertia from the Soviet days.

In Russia's fractured domestic political landscape, the presidency too has often acted as an autonomous institution and as a force in the policy-making process that is separate from the rest of the government. Control of foreign policy in general, regardless of any particular tangible benefit, is an important presidential prerogative.[16] The Persian Gulf, as a region of global importance and interest to all major powers, is automatically an area of interest for the Kremlin, at the very least as a matter of political prestige.

Two other groups deserve to be mentioned among significant Russian players who have a stake in Russian policy in the Gulf: the Jewish community in Russia and the Russophone diaspora in Israel. Contrary to many observers' expectations, Russia has remained home to an active Jewish community. A number of Jewish businessmen achieved a position of considerable prominence and influence in the country's economy and politics. At the same time, the vast Russophone diaspora in Israel has maintained close ties to Russia.[17] The result has been a dynamic Russian-Israeli relationship. Although Jewish-Russian business leaders have not come together in a coherent pro-Israeli lobby, Israel's interest in Russia, paradoxically, has emerged as a potentially important factor in Russian policy in the Gulf and relations with Iran and Iraq. Good relations with Russia are an important domestic political card, which few Israeli politicians can afford not to play, given the strength of the Russian-Israeli electorate.[18] For Russia, with its diminished status in the international arena, good relations with Israel also represent an important goal, given Israel's role as a regional power in the Middle East.

These diverse groups represent rather diverse interests. Russian weapons manufacturers and merchants are guided by the most straightforward and simple goal: they are eager to sell their wares because their market at home is too small to satisfy their appetites for profits or their need to pay hundreds of thousands of workers and their families. Exports are seen as a matter of industry-wide survival. The same logic applies to MINATOM and its relationship with Iran. For both the defense-industrial complex and the nuclear power sector, the zeal to open up new markets is further reinforced by deep-seated suspicions that Russia has long been denied its legitimate access to international markets dominated by Western arms merchants.[19]

Thus, U.S. appeals for restraint in arms sales touch a raw nerve in the defense-industrial community, where such appeals are widely seen as thinly veiled protection of U.S. commercial interests. Resisting these appeals is a matter of both commercial and patriotic interest. In addition, Russian weapons manufacturers have a powerful stake in Iraq. The latter owes Russia $7 billion for past weapons deliveries, which the Russian side still hopes to collect.[20] Beyond that, Iraq is an attractive future market for their wares once the sanctions regime is removed; it has a long tradition of buying Soviet equipment. Both new equipment purchases and contracts to upgrade existing systems are a source of high hopes of Russian defense industrialists and exporters. Coupled with Iraq's ability to finance its purchases with oil revenues, these hopes have resulted in a powerful domestic pro-Iraqi lobby in Russia.

Russian oil companies have a more complicated agenda in the Gulf. Latecomers to the global energy scene as private corporations, Russian oil companies are not major international players and have little to offer to most Gulf oil producers who enjoy long-established business relationships with international oil companies. Russian companies do not possess the technology, business acumen, or easy access to capital to offer to Persian Gulf states.[21] As a result, Russian companies warily view the Gulf as a major competitor in the international oil market. Instability in the Gulf could further exacerbate the latent tensions between Gulf and Russian oil producers. Russian oil companies have long sought to position themselves as the alternative and far more reliable source of energy to key markets, especially in Europe. President Vladimir Putin's visit to Paris for the Russia-EU summit in October 2000 resulted in a new Russia-EU energy partnership with a clear view—at least from the Russian side—to consolidate Russia's position as Europe's premier energy supplier.[22] Russia's success in this area could prove harmful to its relations with Persian Gulf oil exporters. Russian oil interests have an equally wary relationship with the Organization of Petroleum Exporting Countries (OPEC). Reluctant to join it for fear of having to abide by its rules, Russian oil majors have preferred to cooperate with it episodically, depending on their own needs. They have certainly shown little propensity to exercise restraint or sacrifice their own commercial interest for the sake of advancing those of OPEC members.[23]

An important exception in this context is Iraq. For Russian oil companies, Iraq represents an attractive business opportunity; Iraqi oil is a good deal more accessible and cheaper to produce than oil from fields in remote regions of Russia, which have yet to be explored and developed. Russia's special relationship with Saddam Husayn had long put Russian companies in an advantageous position for political, rather than commercial, reasons.[24] There can be little doubt about the political motives behind Iraqi courtship of Russian oil companies and awarding to them of potentially lucrative oil contracts. These motives became all the more transparent when Baghdad cancelled its contract with Lukoil, the largest Russian oil company, after Russia joined the United States in a unanimous Security Council vote for UNSC Resolution 1441 and reports surfaced that Lukoil representatives had held meetings with representatives of the Iraqi opposition.[25]

Still, several Russian oil companies hold potentially lucrative contracts with Iraq. Fully cognizant of the political motivations behind Saddam's decision to award these contracts to their companies, Russian oil industry executives suspect that in the event of regime change in Baghdad, they will be among the losers in the Iraqi oil sweepstakes because Saddam's successors will be more likely to reward their backers with lucrative contracts.[26] These concerns in turn generate further suspicions among Russian executives about the true motives behind the U.S. goal of regime change in Iraq. These suspicions have not prevented Russian oil companies from exploring opportunities in a post-Saddam Iraq. To the contrary, as tensions in the Persian Gulf escalated throughout 2002, Russian corporate interests, through a variety of spokesmen, telegraphed their willingness to trade support for Saddam's regime for an opportunity to do business with a post-Saddam government. In sum, Russian business interests have made it quite clear that Russian acquiescence to U.S.-led anti-Saddam efforts comes with a price tag.[27]

The interest of Russia's professional national security bureaucracy in the Gulf is of a less tangible nature. Lacking a concrete commercial interest, this group has not come to terms with Russia's loss of superpower status. It harbors deep resentment of the United States and its preeminent position in the world and sees it in Russia's national interest to oppose the United States, and to undercut its influence and initiatives in the region regardless of their impact on Russian security or well being. Thus, this group is motivated by traditional, albeit outmoded, geopolitical considerations.

Both the professional national security bureaucracy and the Kremlin have a further interest in the Gulf prompted by the increasing challenge of militant Islam to Russian national security. The war in Chechnya has attracted a good deal of attention in the Islamic world. The Chechen side is reported to have received support from a number of Islamic countries, including Saudi Arabia, in the form of both volunteers and material assistance.[28] Russian authorities have also claimed repeatedly that Osama bin Laden has provided support and training for Chechen fighters. As a result, curbing international Islamic support for the Chechen cause has become an active concern for Russian policy in the Gulf.

In the domestic political context, Russian relations with Iran and Iraq have enhanced the Kremlin's ability to protect itself from Communist-nationalist attacks by showing that under its leadership, Russia indeed is pursuing an independent foreign policy and has not become a lackey of the United States. Hence, undercutting U.S. initiatives on Iraq or defending Russia's right to sell weapons and nuclear technology to Iran have become elements of the Kremlin's domestic political strategy. In addition, the Kremlin has a particular interest in the Gulf because of potential tangible material or political benefits. Control over arms exports and associated financial flows is an important asset for the Kremlin to have at its disposal at times when funding is needed for the conduct of political campaigns or to reward political supporters.[29]

Conflicts of Interests

Russian interests in the Gulf entail considerable contradictions, if only because of the omnivorous nature of Russian foreign policy and the inability of the political elite to coalesce around a shared vision of national interest and priorities. Russian-Iranian relations are particularly full of contradictions. A close commercial relationship involving billions of dollars worth of arms sales and completion of the Bushehr nuclear power plant provides a tangible foundation for the relationship. Moreover, Iran needs Russia as a potential balance to the United States in its standoff with Washington, as well as for the sheer political prestige of having good relations with Moscow, even in its diminished capacity. Russia needs good relations with Iran to maintain an important foothold in the Gulf, where its presence is otherwise quite limited. Lastly, the two may once again join forces in the future to minimize U.S. influence in the Caucasus and Central Asia—the two regions both see as their strategic sphere of influence.

Nonetheless, the potential for Russian-Iranian competition is vast. Russian analysts are not blind to Iran's nuclear ambitions, take them virtually for granted, and voice occasional concerns about their likely impact on Russian security.[30] While both countries' foreign policy establishments have resented U.S. Caspian energy diplomacy, they no longer share a common position on the Caspian. Following substantial new oil discoveries in its sector of the Caspian, Russia has embraced the idea of sectoral division of the sea, which Iran has firmly opposed. How will this potentially serious dispute in the Caspian affect the overall relationship between Moscow and Tehran? Will Russian energy companies pursuing Caspian projects be pitted against Russian arms manufacturers eager to protect their key market? Will the Kremlin be able to adjudicate among them?

Moreover, Moscow's support for the United States in the war on terrorism runs the risk of putting it increasingly at odds with Tehran. For example, Russia's national security establishment is grudgingly coming to terms with the U.S. military presence in Afghanistan and Central Asia as a factor for stability. The same evidently cannot be said about Iran's national security establishment, where the U.S presence in Iran's backyard has added to its sense of encirclement. In addition, in the Israeli-Palestinian conflict, Russian sympathies, influenced heavily by the Chechen experience, lie strongly and visibly with the Israelis, who are perceived as victims of terrorism and allies in the common struggle against militant Islam. Iran is a main sponsor of militant Islamic groups responsible for numerous terrorist attacks against Israel and has sought to supply arms to the Palestinian Authority for use in attacking Israel. This divergence is likely to have a dampening effect on Russian-Iranian relations.

There are also differences over control of future Caspian pipelines and access to the Turkish gas market, where both countries have vast aspirations and ambitious pipeline schemes, and over Russia's conduct of the war in Chechnya. Russia also worries that Tehran will resume support to Islamic extremist movements in the formerly Soviet, predominantly Muslim republics of Central Asia (for example, Tajikistan), which in turn would serve as a back door to influence Russia's Muslim population.

But perhaps the biggest long-term challenge facing their relationship is the prospect of normalized relations between Iran and the United States.

While such a turn of events would in all likelihood be slow and gradual, it would nonetheless begin to erode Russian influence in Iran. With the important exception of weapons and military technology, Russia has little to offer to Iran once its diplomatic isolation is finally broken.

It is not well positioned, for instance, to offer Iran the capital, technology, or managerial know-how it needs to modernize its economy or develop its energy sector. Moreover, while the military-technical relationship may continue for some time, its long-term viability is open to doubt because of Russia's questionable ability to deliver the weapons Iran needs. Russian defense industry, as the rest of the Russian economy, has been starved for investment; its ability to deliver on current contracts is already in doubt. Its ability to sustain production for years to come is even more problematic.[31]

Together, these divergent interests cast doubt over the ability of Russia and Iran to sustain the warm political relationship they have enjoyed in recent years. Indeed, unless Russia and Iran can muster the diplomatic adroitness and political will to sustain their partnership in the face of these many difficult challenges, it is likely to fray as a result of tensions over trade, energy, and military issues. And should an eventual U.S.-Iranian rapprochement materialize, which Russia would see as coming at its expense, the process would be accelerated.

In this context, it is important to note that Iran is in the driver's seat in the bilateral relationship with Russia. Russia has found itself quite literally as a seller in a buyer's market, desperate for Iranian cash. Presently, it has few levers with which it could influence the long-term outlook for the relationship, short of withholding weapons, equipment, and WMD assistance from Iran—a course it appears highly unlikely to adopt, given its current posture of liberal arms sales and military-technological exports to Tehran.[32]

Russian-Iraqi relations seem destined for a more troubled future as well. Should Iraq undergo a regime change and begin the process of returning to the community of nations, including the lifting of the sanctions regime, Russia again would find itself holding few cards. The oil deals promised by Saddam to Russian companies on the basis of obvious political considerations are not likely to be honored by Saddam's successors, who probably would be equally reluctant to honor the dictator's $7 billion debt to Russia due to both political reasons and far more pressing demands. Russia has little to offer Iraq as a source of capital, technology, and know-how once it embarks on the path of reconstruction. It is thus likely to find itself marginalized once again.

The Outlook

Notwithstanding the tensions outlined in the preceding section, Russian behavior is unlikely to change significantly in the near term on its own, without external pressures or stimuli. Domestic weakness will remain a singular feature of Russian foreign policy, which will be vulnerable to powerful domestic interests. These pressures will in effect preclude Russia from developing a coherent sense of strategic priorities and orchestrating a comeback in the Middle East as a major strategic player.

Russia is a marginal player in Persian Gulf affairs. Its main role is that of an eager and indiscriminate arms supplier—the role it has assumed not by choice but out of weakness. Its long-term success in reversing its fortunes is closely tied to its ability to wean itself from the habit of arms exports and to undertake structural reforms. Given the domestic political context, such a turn of events is unlikely, signaling in turn that Russia will remain a presence in the Persian Gulf arms bazaar for as long as it will be able to find buyers. In the long run, absent a sudden change in the domestic political environment in Russia, its role as an arms supplier will gradually atrophy due to growing technological obsolescence. In sum, with the notable exception of WMD proliferation, Russia is likely to create headaches for U.S. policy but will not pose a major challenge to U.S. interests or policy in the Gulf, including the use of U.S. military force to remove Saddam Husayn from power.

China

China's economic development has been the top priority on Beijing's national agenda since the late 1970s and will be the driving force behind its strategy toward the Persian Gulf region in the years ahead. The economic growth of the past 2 decades has spurred China's growing demand for energy resources. In response to dwindling domestic supply, China has turned to the Persian Gulf to satisfy the nation's economic needs. As a result, energy security has become a central component of its national security. At the same time, China's economic success has augmented its "comprehensive national power," which in Chinese strategic thinking encompasses a broad range of economic, political, diplomatic, and military capabilities. Beijing has slowly maximized these hard-earned assets to exert its influence in the Gulf region.

Nevertheless, as Chinese activism in Gulf affairs increases, Beijing will have to compete with other major players with equally compelling stakes in the region. In particular, how China's security policies in the

Gulf dovetail or conflict with American interests could have a major impact on the Middle East. It is almost certain that Chinese and American interests will sometimes collide, leading to heightened competition and Sino-American friction. At the same time, Washington and Beijing share common interests in promoting stability and access to energy supplies. It remains unclear how Beijing has prioritized its interests, goals, and strategies in the region. Understanding the potentially divergent and convergent U.S. and Chinese interests in the Gulf region will be an increasingly important task for both nations.

Geopolitical Ambitions

The promise of major geopolitical shifts in the international system has motivated Beijing to play a more prominent role in the Gulf region. Many Chinese strategists predicted throughout the 1990s that the international structure would devolve from an American-centric unipolar world toward multipolarity. According to their forecasts, as American preeminence declines, other major states (including China) would rise to become coequals.[33] Numerous Chinese observers have noted that America's unchallenged global power has already shown signs of decay in the Middle East, as manifested by widespread Arab resentment toward American support for Israel, America's unpopular dual containment policy against Iraq and Iran, and the more assertive EU role in the region.[34] The Gulf region figures prominently in Chinese strategic thinking as a stage for geopolitical competition against American hegemony. To be sure, the American-led NATO operation in Kosovo forced the Chinese government to reassess the international security environment and aroused alarm in some quarters that the United States might reverse the trend toward multipolarity. America's success to date in Operation *Enduring Freedom* has likely reinforced these doubts. Nonetheless, Chinese analysts still concur that multipolarity is an irreversible trend and differ only on the pace of the changes in the international structure.

As Beijing seeks a more active role in the Gulf, how will it translate its ambitions into action? China's relative weakness in influence and military power compared to its Western competitors will largely dictate Chinese behavior in the contest for influence. China will solicit the goodwill of friends and adversaries of the United States to counterbalance American influence in the region and can exploit deep resentments in the Middle East, particularly in Iran and Iraq, toward Washington's policies in the region. China could also try to play the role of a regional balancer between the GCC states and their archenemies, Iran and Iraq, and will no doubt exert its power in the UN Security Council to influence critical decisions on the fate of the region.

In bilateral terms, China has fostered closer ties with Iran, Iraq, and Saudi Arabia. Beijing regards Iran as an indisputable regional power and an indispensable partner for achieving China's goals in the Persian Gulf. Both countries share a determination to oppose American hegemony there.[35] Thus, China will look to Iran as a major bulwark against American influence in the region. Since military ties blossomed during the Iran-Iraq war, Beijing's support for Baghdad remains strong. As the sanctions regime against Iraq has slowly eroded, China, along with Russia and France, has patiently chipped away at the UN edifice. As the largest producer of oil, Saudi Arabia has become an increasingly important partner for China in the Persian Gulf, although in the future, a larger portion of Chinese needs for imported oil could be met from Central Asian and Iranian supplies.

Nonetheless, in China's hierarchy of national security interests, challenging American power in the Persian Gulf remains a relatively low priority. Security concerns closer to home already consume most of China's energy and resources. The uncertainties of the Korean Peninsula, anxieties over Japan's future path, and the unresolved Taiwan question are among the many issues that require constant vigilance. China also recognizes that the U.S. military presence in the Gulf region ensures stability. An American withdrawal would almost certainly result in major regional upheaval and possibly conflict that would prove much more harmful to Beijing's interests than the current status quo. China simply cannot afford the strategic vacuum that would result from a U.S. departure from the Gulf. As long as China cannot supplant the United States or replicate its stabilizing role, Beijing will not attempt to alter the prevailing balance of power in the region.

The Centrality of Energy Security

Historically, China's strategic interest in the Gulf region has been negligible. During the Cold War, the Middle East was a peripheral arena of ideological confrontation for China.[36] In the 1990s, China's relative indifference dissipated as energy security began to demand strategic attention in Beijing. This shift in attitude resulted from China's continuing economic success, which unleashed an insatiable appetite for energy resources to fuel the nation's growth. Tremendous surges in demand for energy supplies have slowly outstripped China's declining domestic output. In 1993, China became a net importer of oil for the first time. By 2000, China imported 1.4 million barrels per day, constituting 30 percent of its total oil consumption. In the late 1990s, the Middle East provided approximately half of the oil imports, and that share will likely grow.[37] Given China's longstanding insistence on self-reliance, the growing proportion of foreign-supplied oil, particularly from the Persian Gulf, triggers acute anxieties. Moreover, the volatility of the Gulf region further heightens Chinese fears of unexpected, large-scale disruptions to energy supplies. As a result, energy security in the Gulf has become a central component of China's economy and its strategic thinking.

The dim prospects for exploiting alternative sources of energy have exacerbated China's unenviable position, ensuring that its dependence on Middle Eastern energy supplies and the attendant insecurities will only grow in the coming years. China's indigenous energy resources are limited; its most productive oil fields in the east are already drying up, and extracting oil reserves from Xinjiang Province poses daunting technological and political challenges.[38] The promise of oil transported from the heartland of Eurasia to China through continental pipelines remains in the distant future due to formidable technical, logistical, financial, and political obstacles. In addition, oil exploration in the South China Sea has thus far yielded disappointing results, and the potential costs of exploiting the seabed there may outweigh the benefits.

From Beijing's perspective, America's unrivaled influence and substantial military presence in the Middle East represent a two-edged sword for China's energy security. On the one hand, China benefits from the stability that U.S. military forces bring to the region without incurring any costs. On the other hand, Beijing fears that it could be held hostage to American threats to deny China's access to oil during confrontations with the United States over other disputes.[39] With the rise of Chinese nationalism, the notion that the supply of oil could be subject to Washington's goodwill chafes Beijing and adds to its insecurity. However, the practicality of an oil embargo is highly questionable. Cutting off oil supplies to a major power would be politically difficult to justify to the international community. In addition, as the current sanctions against Iraq demonstrate, monitoring supply routes that span the Persian Gulf, the Indian Ocean, the South China Sea, and the Western Pacific would be a logistical nightmare. The attendant short-term shock to prices might also hurt more oil-dependent allies such as Japan. In short, Chinese concerns regarding America's military dominance in the Gulf are largely psychological; short of a major Sino-American war, there is very little compelling rationale for Washington to block the flow of oil to China. Nevertheless, for Beijing, energy security in the Persian Gulf demonstrates both the benefits of American power and China's potential vulnerabilities to U.S. global dominance.

Arms Sales to the Gulf

China's pattern of arms sales and related technology transfers, particularly in the area of WMD, have often unnerved Gulf Arab regimes and put Beijing directly at odds with America's nonproliferation policy. Beijing has delivered arms to prominent rogue states (Iran and Iraq) and moderate Gulf states (Saudi Arabia and Kuwait). These weapons include artillery pieces, a guided missile boat, surface-to-air missiles (SAMs), and antiship missiles that give Iran a greater potential to threaten shipping and U.S. naval forces passing through the Strait of Hormuz.[40] More worrying has been the growing trend in the past 2 decades of Chinese exports of NBC technologies and related delivery systems. For example, China has delivered to Iran entire dual-use factories and supplies that can produce chemical and biological weapons; nuclear technology and know-how for civilian nuclear programs; and technological assistance in the indigenous production of long-range ballistic and cruise missiles.

Given the genuine threat that rogue nations pose to U.S. forward-deployed forces in the Persian Gulf and regional friends and allies, such proliferation behavior has been a major source of contention in Sino-American relations. China has repeatedly broken pledges to the United States not to violate arms control agreements.[41] Why would China risk undermining an arguably far more critical bilateral relationship with a superpower for what appears to be short-term gains?

Potential financial benefits motivate China to pursue a relatively lax arms sales policy toward the region. The Middle East, one of the most militarized regions in the world and the top destination for foreign weapons, has been a lucrative arms market for China. Regional rivalries between the GCC states, Iran, and Iraq, as well as intra-GCC competition, have spurred demand. Because China has been willing to proliferate particularly sensitive military technologies and weapons of mass destruction, those denied hardware from the West have thus turned to Beijing. This pattern of interaction has enabled Beijing to capture a niche market that other governments have been unwilling to penetrate. Beyond the lure of profit, China's strategic interests benefit from arms sales. Anticipating the demise of America's dual containment policy, Beijing has relied on proliferation to Iran and Iraq in the hopes of earning preferential terms on oil concessions or to dissuade attempts to deny access to oil. Conversely, some Gulf regimes have also exploited the promise of hard currency to secure political compromises from China.

   Most important, arms sales are tied directly to broader developments in Sino-American relations. Arms sales complement Beijing's geopolitical maneuvers to undermine American standing in the Middle East; they not only cement ties with major oil producers in the region but also represent powerful symbolic gestures of defiance against U.S. dominance. Similarly, the Gulf states have turned to China to signal their displeasure at certain U.S. policies or when American support is not forthcoming. Beijing has also relied on the threat of proliferation as a counterweight to U.S. policies that threaten China's interests (for example, U.S. arms sales to Taiwan).

   While Chinese arms sales to the Gulf region have served both as an end (profit) and a means (enhancing its status while undermining American influence) to achieve Beijing's strategic objectives, the proliferation of weaponry has thus far demonstrated limited utility. China has made only modest inroads, which peaked during the Iran-Iraq War. Despite the financial appeal of cheap Chinese weaponry, they do not provide the level of sophistication that many Gulf states have come to expect. China has never been a serious competitor with Western suppliers in profitable big-ticket conventional items, such as modern fighter aircraft. Since the late 1980s, the transfer of Chinese conventional arms has steadily declined. From 1987 to 1997, the value of arms sales contracts to the Middle East collapsed from $1.5 billion to $400 million in 1997 constant prices;[42] from 1993 to 2000, the value of arms deliveries in current U.S. dollars to the Middle East region declined from $1.2 billion to $800 million.[43] During this same period, military sales to Iran dropped from $900 million to $400 million.[44] As a result, the revenues generated from arms sales worldwide now account for a negligible percentage of China's overall export earnings. Moreover, while much of the export earnings are invested in Chinese military modernization, the persistent rise in the defense budget in the past few years has reduced the relative importance of the benefits of Chinese arms sales.

   It remains somewhat unclear what role arms sales will play in China's overall strategy in the future. It is possible, for example, that China might become concerned that selling WMD-related weapons to rogue states with undisguised ambitions for regional dominance is highly destabilizing to the region. Tehran, equipped with NBC capabilities, might be able to coerce its neighbors or directly threaten American forces in the region. Such nightmare scenarios, particularly protracted conflicts, would directly impact China's energy security concerns. Furthermore, China's arms transfers risk provoking the United States and the imposition of American sanctions that could strain bilateral relations and harm Chinese commercial interests.

Washington has often relied on the blunt instrument of economic sanctions to deter or punish proliferation behavior. Finally, Chinese sales of advanced conventional weaponry to Iraq and Iran undermine its image
among moderate Arab regimes, which are equally crucial suppliers of oil
for China. Hence, arms sales represent a double-edged sword for Beijing.

Implications for U.S. Policy

These three main drivers of Chinese policy in the Gulf—geopolitics,
energy security, and arms sales—reflect disparate agendas that often clash
with one another. As noted above, the potential instability that WMD
sales could unleash in the region would prove harmful to China's energy
security. It is doubtful, in addition, that an ambitious power armed with
nuclear weapons would be any less ambivalent toward or more constrained by China. Moreover, rising tensions in Sino-American relations
or American retaliation in the form of sanctions would hurt China's
strategic and economic interests.

Beijing must therefore carefully weigh the tradeoffs between these
impulses behind China's Gulf policy and prioritize its policies accordingly.
How might China prioritize its policy agenda? The financial and political
benefits of arms sales have been ambiguous at best. While fiery rhetoric
often accompanies discussions of multipolarity, China does not yet possess the capacity to challenge American interests worldwide. It would
appear, then, that energy security offers the most tangible, immediate
benefits to China. Its national comprehensive power depends largely on
economic vitality. Moreover, with the decline of ideology, economic
success has become the only viable tool for maintaining the legitimacy of
the Chinese Communist Party as well as domestic political and social
stability. Consequently, the energy resources to fuel China's economy will
ultimately exert greater influence over China's Gulf policy.

What are the implications of China's obsession with energy security
for U.S. policy? The preceding assessment of Chinese interests suggests that
China's threat to American interests will be low to moderate in the next 10
to 15 years. While China is wary of America's potential capability to exercise
a military veto over Chinese access to energy resources, there is significant
overlap of interests between Beijing and Washington. Energy security is vital
to China and America's allies who depend on Gulf oil. China recognizes that
the United States has and will continue to play a stabilizing political and military role in the region. Accordingly, China will likely continue to support
some U.S. policies, such as preventing the rise of a hegemon. In the event of
another Gulf War, China probably would not openly endorse any coalition

action nor actively resist it in the Security Council (a position it took during *Desert Storm*). Beijing's energy security stakes are sufficiently high that China would oppose the forcible occupation of vast swaths of territory in the Arabian Peninsula by either Iraq or Iran. It is doubtful, though, that Chinese opposition would go beyond rhetoric to include military participation in or support for a U.S.-led coalition operation.

There are those in the United States who worry that China might be able to intervene militarily in the Gulf in the future.[45] How plausible is such a scenario? China has no doubt embarked on an aggressive naval modernization program that could significantly improve its ability to project power beyond its shores. However, several geopolitical and military considerations would severely constrain China's military option in the region. First, tremendous opportunity costs are associated with an ambitious venture into the Persian Gulf that would amount to a strategic overreach. Over the next 10 to 15 years, China must contend with many other critical security concerns that are likely to preoccupy its attention. The volatility of cross-strait relations, dangers on the Korean Peninsula, the uncertain future path of Japan, and the rise of India on China's southern flank are just some of the major issues that will continue to dominate Chinese military strategy and thinking. China is not likely to expend military resources for the Gulf at the expense of the above contingencies. An expeditionary force is simply incompatible with China's narrower security interests, particularly concerning the unresolved Taiwan question.

Second, China does not have the military capability to enforce its will in the Gulf. Most of China's more modern surface combatants and submarines are based in the East Sea Fleet for a Taiwan Strait contingency. The ships of the South Sea Fleet only have a limited capacity to patrol the South China Sea. Moreover, China possesses few modern ships and naval aviation that can perform the necessary tasks of a blue-water navy. Ultimately, China will need to develop and deploy several aircraft carrier groups to project meaningful naval power in the Persian Gulf. So far, Beijing has not embarked on such an ambitious modernization plan. Even if China pursues such an option in the next decade, most of the carriers would likely be dedicated to a cross-strait contingency if the Taiwan question remains unresolved. In other words, Beijing recognizes that there is little that China could do to oppose U.S. military preponderance in the Gulf, further undercutting the rationale for developing force projection capabilities for the region.

There are several scenarios that could alter China's calculus toward the region. First, the analysis above suggests that America's political and military position in the Gulf is a major determinant of how China will define its long-term role in the region. Should Washington falter, the strategic vacuum in the wake of a U.S. withdrawal could bring about tremendous instability that would harm China's economic interests. In such a scenario, Beijing would then be confronted with a particularly acute quandary if it did not possess the capabilities to assert or defend its interests in the Gulf. Second, U.S. relations with Iran and Iraq over the next decade could fundamentally reshape the political map of the region for China. Should a U.S.-Iranian rapprochement come to fruition, China's ability to pit Tehran against Washington would diminish significantly. Third, internal changes in Iraq, Iran, and the GCC states could have major policy consequences for Beijing. The triumph of reformers in Iran or the rise of a moderate post-Saddam regime in Iraq could limit China's ability to maneuver against the United States.

The war against terrorism in the aftermath of September 11 embodies all three Chinese concerns above. China's support for U.S. military operations in Afghanistan, a decision that would have been unthinkable given Beijing's vehement opposition to American interventions abroad, reflects a fundamental realignment of strategic priorities. As a victim of previous terrorist attacks from Muslim separatist movements in Xinjiang, China has a stake in supporting the United States. Moreover, a successful operation that brings stability to the region would allow Beijing to enjoy continued access to energy supplies. However, there are limits to China's acquiescence. It hopes to see the U.S. war against terrorism contained in Afghanistan. In strictly geopolitical terms, the collapse of Saddam Husayn's regime would be a major blow to China's quest for influence in the region. As such, the potential for the United States to settle old scores and to alter the balance of power in the Gulf no doubt worries the Chinese. For these reasons, the level of Chinese collaboration in this campaign is likely to be limited.

In terms of concrete policy options, the United States should hedge against China's challenges in the Gulf and explore opportunities for minimizing bilateral tensions and objectionable Chinese actions while promoting cooperation where the United States and China have shared interests. While Chinese arms sales behavior has improved, it is still the most worrisome component of Beijing's strategy. Recognizing that it will be extremely difficult to obtain a complete halt to Chinese arms sales to the region, the United States should be prepared to wield a big stick to deter those Chinese nonproliferation activities that pose a real threat to regional and U.S. national security. Differentiating among Chinese arms sales in this manner may in fact improve U.S. credibility in trying to dissuade truly destabilizing Chinese transfers.

Washington should also undertake a series of initiatives with an eye toward the longer-term future. The United States could play a potentially important role in dampening the pressures of oil dependence and the associated incentives for Beijing to exert its influence in the Gulf. For example, the Russian Far East contains tremendous energy potential for China. Washington should encourage multilateral efforts—including Japan, South Korea, China, and Russia—to explore, exploit, and share the resources in Russia as an alternative to the Gulf. Some have floated the idea of regional strategic oil reserves shared among the powers in Northeast Asia. Such initiatives not only serve the economic interests of all parties involved but would also function as indirect confidence-building measures that have hitherto been absent in the region. This lack of regional cooperation on energy security points to the need for regular high-level dialogue among the powers of Northeast Asia.

More broadly, senior U.S. Government and Chinese officials should meet regularly to discuss the Persian Gulf as part of a broader, sustained, and more substantive bilateral dialogue on global security issues. Such a dialogue may go a long way toward harmonizing American and Chinese views on the role that U.S. military power plays in the Gulf in advancing our common interest in the uninterrupted flow of Gulf oil. In parallel with these policy-level discussions, moreover, the U.S. and Chinese militaries should begin a dialogue on peacetime military cooperation in the Gulf. For example, Chinese show-the-flag deployments would signal Chinese resolve, along with the United States and the West, to protect Gulf oil supplies, and there may be some practical steps the United States could take to facilitate these activities.

Conclusion

The involvement of outside powers in the Gulf scene creates two sets of problems for U.S. regional security strategy. First, it opens up opportunities for regional states to balance American influence by appealing to European countries, Russia, or China. Indeed, in many cases, the external great powers may be just as dissatisfied with the regional status quo as the regional rogues are themselves. Baghdad and Tehran might find support and encouragement for their efforts to overturn the status quo from great powers looking to remake the Gulf political order more to their liking. In short, adding more players to the Gulf mix could easily encourage the more adventurous tendencies of Gulf rogues.

Second, and potentially of much greater significance, some of these great powers could furnish Gulf states with highly sophisticated weaponry. For all of the reasons discussed in chapter four, even highly advanced weaponry is not likely to reverse the current balance of power so favorable to the United States. However, as suggested in the previous chapter, large numbers of cutting-edge weaponry (especially when coupled with mature WMD capabilities) could suddenly make new strategies for aggression more feasible.

In particular, if Iraq or Iran acquired large numbers of advanced antiship, antitank, and antiaircraft missiles and possessed a well-developed WMD capability, they might be able to successfully carry out a limited-war strategy. If the weapons in question were the coming generation of brilliant weapons—which effectively identify and track targets and guide themselves, thereby obviating the need for any real skill on the part of the operator (and do so at stand-off ranges, obviating the need for maneuver or combined arms operations)—this could render irrelevant many of the crippling problems Iraq and Iran have experienced in combat.

Even possessing large numbers of the current generation of Russian or European SAMs, antitank missiles, antiship missiles, and air-to-air missiles would make Iraq or Iran a far more dangerous foe. If coupled with a WMD capability that they could reasonably expect would deter the United States from escalating, such a capability might allow for successful land-grab-type operations. For instance, if Iraq had access to such weapons, it might calculate that it could use its standing forces to overrun Iraqi Kurdistan or possibly even Kuwait. It could then rely on a wall of advanced SAMs and antitank missiles to defeat the inevitable American counterattack while its weapons of mass destruction would make Washington wary of escalating, either horizontally or vertically. In effect, it would allow a 21st-century version of Anwar Sadat's October 1973 strategy, in which Egypt seized a bridgehead in Sinai and then defended it against Israeli counterattacks with a wall of missiles. Militarily, Israel found a way to win in 1973, but politically Sadat won the Sinai back. A future Iranian or Iraqi leader possessing large numbers of advanced munitions might believe that he could do even better than Sadat.

Its immense power notwithstanding, the threats and challenges that are likely to confront the United States in the Persian Gulf over the next decade are beyond our capacity to handle without the help of others. In the near term, European support for U.S. military action against Iraq, while not essential militarily (except perhaps for Turkey), would confer much greater political and international legitimacy on the use of U.S. military force and help ensure a substantial European contribution to the postwar reconstruction of Iraq and a stable regional order. Additionally, Europe can play a critical role, in coordination with the United States, in alleviating the underlying causes of terrorism. European restraint in the transfer of dual-use technology to Iraq and Iran would also help to disrupt and delay efforts by both countries to develop WMD and long-range ballistic missiles. Russian and Chinese cooperation in the Gulf, especially with respect to the sale of advanced conventional weapons to Iraq and Iran, will be an important factor in maintaining a favorable regional military balance as sanctions continue to evaporate. More importantly, both Russia and China have enormous potential to destabilize the region if they continue to aid and abet Iranian and, in the future, Iraqi WMD programs—or if they help both countries in overcoming the deployment of U.S. missile defenses.

Europe, Russia, and China have important stakes in the Gulf, and their policies and interests will not always coincide with American desiderata. It is unrealistic, therefore, to expect these three centers of power to accept U.S. initiatives unquestioningly. That said, Europe, China, and, to a lesser degree, Russia depend on U.S. power and leadership to protect important interests in the region. Furthermore, many of their differences with the United States can be muted through more intense and regular dialogue on issues that affect common interests. Simply put, over the next decade and beyond, the United States will find it easier to accomplish its objectives in the Gulf acting in cooperation and partnership with these countries than acting alone. Dealing with the region's intractable problems on a multilateral basis will require negotiation and compromise and may even, at times, constrain U.S. freedom of action. But the benefits of such cooperation, especially insofar as they reduce the political, diplomatic, and material burdens of U.S. exposure in the region, outweigh the costs. Perhaps more importantly, unilateral U.S. policies not only will founder on the shoals of regional realities but are also likely to hasten the day when Europe, Russia, and China concert their efforts to constrain the exercise of American power and to thwart U.S. diplomatic initiatives.

Notes

[1] The authors acknowledge the contributions to this chapter by Kenneth Pollack and Toshi Yoshihara, senior staff member at the Institute for Foreign Policy Analysis, Cambridge, MA. For more extensive discussion of Chinese policy toward the Persian Gulf, on which this chapter draws heavily,

see Toshi Yoshihara and Richard D. Sokolsky, "The United States and China in the Persian Gulf: Challenges and Opportunities," *The Fletcher Forum of World Affairs* 26, no. 1 (Winter/Spring 2002), 63–77.

[2] For a good overview of these interests and U.S.-European relations in the Gulf, from which much of the discussion here is drawn, see Simon Serfaty, "Bridging the Gap Across the Atlantic: Europe and the United States in the Persian Gulf," *The Middle East Journal* 52, no. 3 (Summer 1998).

[3] Indeed, as one prominent European observer has noted, many European leaders hope to build the European Union as a counterweight to America's global political, economic, cultural, and military influence. See Charles Moore, "Our Friends in Europe," *The Wall Street Journal*, March 8, 2002. Moore is the editor-in-chief of the *London Daily Telegraph*.

[4] See Michael Gordon, "Cheney Rejects Criticism by Allies Over Stand on Iraq," *The New York Times*, February 16, 2002.

[5] See Wolfgang Ischinger, "When West and West Collide," *The Washington Times*, March 27, 2002. Ischinger is German Ambassador to the United States.

[6] For a perceptive American perspective on European attitudes toward the use of force and international order, see Robert Kagan, "Power and Weakness," *Policy Review*, June 2002.

[7] See Philip H. Gordon, "Iraq: The Transatlantic Debate," European Institute for Security Studies Occasional Paper 39 (December 2002), accessed at <http://www.iss-eu.org>.

[8] Christopher Patten as quoted in Evelyn Iritani, "U.S. Urged to Preserve Coalition," *Los Angeles Times*, February 20, 2002.

[9] See Joseph Fitchett, "Pentagon in a League of Its Own," *International Herald Tribune*, February 4, 2002.

[10] See Karl Vick, "After Calls on Turkey, U.S. Put on Hold," *The Washington Post*, January 8, 2003.

[11] Gordon, "Iraq: The Transatlantic Debate," 20.

[12] Ibid.

[13] Unless otherwise noted, this discussion draws extensively on Eugene B. Rumer, *Dangerous Drift: Russian Policy in the Middle East* (Washington, DC: The Washington Institute for Near East Policy, 2000).

[14] Oleg Zamyslovskiy, "Gendirektor 'Promeksporta' Andrei Belyaninov: Vosstanovit' Ob'yom Proizvodstva Vooruzheniy" ("Promeksport Director General Andrei Belyaninov: Restore the Level of Arms Production"), *Nezavisimaya Gazeta*, October 27, 2000; Craig Covault, "Russian Air Force Faces Deepening Crisis," *Aviation Week and Space Technology*, March 5, 2001; Pavel Felgenhauer, "The Lure of Arms for Iran," *The Moscow Times*, November 30, 2000.

[15] A. Vaganov, "Atomnyye Manevry" ("Atomic Maneuvers"), *Nezavisimaya Gazeta*, March 21, 1998. See also Rumer, *Dangerous Drift*, 19–20.

[16] This point is reflected first and foremost in the importance attached to personal diplomacy by Boris Yeltsin and Vladimir Putin and the emphasis placed by both leaders on cultivating personal relationships with foreign counterparts.

[17] One in six Israelis is reported to be of ex-Soviet origin.

[18] See Rumer, *Dangerous Drift*, 45–47.

[19] Vadim Solov'yov, "S–300 Na Beregu Persidskogo Zaliva" ("S–300 in the Persian Gulf"), *Nezavisimoye Voyennoye Obozreniye*, March 23, 2001.

[20] OMRI Daily Digest, March 6, 1997.

[21] Yakov Pappe, "Neftyanaya i Gazovaya Diplomatiya Rossii" ("Russia's Oil and Gas Diplomacy"), *Pro et Contra* (Summer 1997).

[22] Accessed at <http://www.europa.eu.int/comm/energy_transport/en/lpi_en_3.html>.

[23] Viktor Bezborodov, "Chernaya Vodka Rossii" ("Russia's Black Vodka"), accessed at <www.SMI.ru>, November 16, 2000; Reuters, "Official: Russia Won't Offer Cuts to OPEC," *The Moscow Times*, October 29, 2001.

[24] Ol'ga Yevgen'yeva, "Irakskuyu Neft v Moskve Uzhe Podelili" ("Iraqi Oil has Already been Divvied up in Moscow"), *Nezavisimaya Gazeta*, December 16, 1999; Anna Raff, "Envoy: Russia to Earn Billions in Iraq," *The Moscow Times*, August 17, 2001.

[25] "Khusein Nakazal Lukoil za Svyazi S Irakskoy Oppozitsiey" ("Husayn Punished Lukoil for Connections with Iraqi Opposition"), *Nezavisimaya Gazeta*, December 18, 2002.

[26] Interviews in Moscow with Russian oil company executives and analysts, April 2002.

[27] "Khordorkovskiy: U.S. Must Pay for Iraq Support," Reuters, October 23, 2002; "Lukoil Gets Guarantees over Iraq," *The Moscow Times,* October 7, 2002; "My Dolzhny Zashchishchyat' v Irake Rossiyskiy Biznes," accessed at <www.Grani.Ru>, September 6, 2002.

[28] RFE/RL Newsline, March 30, 31, 1999.

[29] Reuben F. Johnson, "Notes of an Idler: Scrambling Arms Export Agencies," *The Moscow Times*, May 12, 2000; Konstantin Makienko, "Torgovat' Oruzhiyem Budut Lyudi Prezidenta" ("The President's People Will Trade Arms"), accessed at <www.VESTI.ru>, November 21, 2000.

[30] See Rumer, *Dangerous Drift*, 61–64.

[31] "Takikh Kontraktov u Rossii Bol'she Ne Budet" ("Russia Will Not Get Such Contracts Anymore"), accessed at <www.VESTI.ru>, December 28, 2000; Fred Weir, "Can Russia Deliver on Arms Sales?" *The Christian Science Monitor*, November 29, 2000.

[32] Judith Ingram, "Moscow Formalizes Arms Deal with Iran," *The Moscow Times*, October 3, 2001.

[33] Michael Pillsbury, *China Debates the Future Security Environment* (Washington, DC: National Defense University Press, 2000).

[34] Huai Chengbo, "Where Has US Diplomacy in the Middle East Gone Wrong?" *Liaowang (International Commentary)*, February 28, 1998, in Foreign Broadcast Information Service, February 28, 1998.

[35] John Calabrese, "China and the Persian Gulf: Energy and Security," *The Middle East Journal*, 362.

[36] See P.R. Kumaraswamy, "Introduction," in *China and the Middle East: The Quest for Influence*, ed. P.R. Kumaraswamy (New Delhi: Sage Publications, 1999), 11–19; Jiang Chen, *From Ideology to Pragmatism: An Analysis of China's Policies Toward the Middle East* (Milwaukee: University of Wisconsin, 1993); and Lillian Craig Harris, *China Considers the Middle East* (London: I.B. Tauris and Company, 1993).

[37] Ji Guoxing, "Energy Security: A View from China," *PacNet* no. 25 (June 25, 1999).

[38] Thomas M. Kane and Lawrence W. Serewicz, "China's Hunger: The Consequences of a Rising Demand for Food and Energy," *Parameters* 31, no. 3 (Autumn 2001), 67.

[39] Washington would consider such an extreme measure only in a wartime scenario, such as a major war in the Taiwan Strait.

[40] Richard F. Grimmit, *Conventional Arms Transfers to Developing Nations, 1993–2000* (Washington, DC: Congressional Research Service, August 2001), 66.

[41] Amy Svitak, "Senator: U.S. Must Stick To Satellite Ban on China," *Defense News*, July 23–29, 2001, 8.

[42] Bureau of Verification and Compliance, Department of State, *World Military Expenditures and Arms Transfers 1998* (Washington, DC: Department of State, August 2000), 174.

[43] Grimmit, 53.

[44] Ibid., 58.

[45] Kane and Serewicz, 66.

Chapter Seven

Policy Implications and Recommendations

Richard D. Sokolsky and Joseph McMillan

Over the next decade, conflicting pressures for continuity and change will buffet the U.S. military posture in the Persian Gulf, whether or not regime change occurs in Iraq. If Saddam Husayn survives, maintaining deterrence and U.S. security commitments will require effective forward deployed forces and the capability to project power rapidly and decisively in the region. However, sustaining the military requirements of a long-term strategy of containment and deterrence will subject the United States to mounting pressures to lower its military profile in the region, especially in Saudi Arabia. If Saddam is removed from power and replaced by either a stable, pro-American government or one that remains hostile to American interests, the United States will also need to make significant adjustments in its forward presence posture in an environment that has been unsettled by war and possibly turmoil in Iraq and the lower Persian Gulf. The same is also true if a post-Saddam regime emerges that, while friendly to American interests, is nonetheless weak and unable to establish its control over a fractious country. How should the United States think about its long-term strategy and presence under these uncertain and unpredictable circumstances?

If Saddam Survives

The future of Saddam Husayn's Iraq will be the most critical variable in determining the evolution of the U.S. military presence in the region. As long as Iraq constitutes a threat to American interests in the Gulf, the United States has little choice but to maintain the capability to deter or defeat that threat with a combination of in-theater and rapidly deployable forces. The Clinton administration decision to deal with Iraqi defiance of United Nations Security Council resolutions through a policy of containment has, until the recent U.S. military buildup in the region, driven the

United States to maintain the status quo in its force presence rather than adopt a more sustainable concept of Gulf security at reduced levels of presence, as was envisioned immediately after Operation *Desert Storm*. Under present conditions, therefore, the U.S. military footprint in the Gulf is determined by the concept of operations for military operations against Iraq.

A decision not to use U.S. military force to evict Saddam in favor of continuing long-term containment must confront several realities: first, sanctions will soon be all but impossible to enforce; second, Iraq will eventually acquire nuclear weapons and longer-range ballistic missiles; third, the U.S. military presence in the region, especially Saudi Arabia, is a source of growing resentment, imposes a mounting domestic liability for the Saudi royal family, and impedes political reform and long-term stability. Finally, there is a growing strategic divergence between how the United States and some of its Gulf state partners perceive regional threats and security requirements: some would prefer in varying degrees that the United States return to the role of off-shore protector; in contrast, the United States remains heavily dependent on forward deployed forces for deterrence and defense. As a result of these factors, the political and military risks to the U.S. force posture in the region are likely to grow, and efforts to maintain the status quo will only exacerbate these dangers. Maintaining long-term containment of Iraq under these circumstances would require a much larger and open-ended U.S. military presence than it currently maintains—one that might be more than the local traffic will bear in most of the Gulf Cooperation Council (GCC) states.

Consequently, if the United States reaffirms the strategy of containment, it will need to think creatively about how to sustain its military component over the long haul. The challenge is to create a new posture for peacetime presence and wartime reinforcement that supports the execution of U.S. defense strategy without creating an unsustainable footprint in the region or draining the overall U.S. force posture of too many forces and resources. This tension can be effectively managed by realigning U.S. forces in the Gulf states, taking advantage of new basing concepts, enhancing the combat capabilities of forward deployed forces, diversifying patterns of deployment, giving higher priority to expanded prepositioning, and investing new energy into expanding multilateral security cooperation. Equally important, the successful creation of a spearhead force and other improvements in U.S. rapid force projection capability would help to alleviate pressures to maintain continuously larger combat forces in the Gulf as well as large, inflexible reinforcement plans if the Iraqi and Iranian military threats continue to grow.

Realigning Forces

While the U.S. forward presence cannot and should not be eliminated or even significantly reduced as long as a hostile Iraqi regime remains in place, it can and should be made less visible, and less seemingly permanent, than it is today. In the short term, to minimize political risks, changes in the size and configuration of U.S. forward deployed forces will need to be carried out incrementally since technological advances in U.S. force projection capabilities will not be in hand for some time. In the longer run, as the U.S. military transforms and political constraints on large stationed forces intensify, it should be possible to accelerate the pace of change because the United States will be able to bring overwhelming force to bear on the battlefield without having to rely on a substantial permanent presence in the theater.

In the near term, the focal point of force realignment is inevitably Saudi Arabia, given the central role it plays in U.S. regional strategy, its size and importance, and the considerable discontent in both the United States and Saudi Arabia over how the U.S. military presence there is handled. A key question is, how much reduction is enough? The United States operates out of only one major base in the Kingdom, which constrains realignment options. Are there less tangible ways of underscoring the American commitment to Saudi security that would not, at the same time, compromise deterrence and U.S. combat capabilities?

Undoubtedly, more can be done in other GCC countries. However, there are political and physical limits on how much of the military burden they can pick up from Saudi Arabia, including in such traditionally U.S.-friendly countries as Kuwait and Bahrain, both of which have experienced an upsurge in anti-American sentiment and Islamist opposition. In the immediate future, the United States is wisely pursuing Qatar as the most attractive alternative to Saudi Arabia for additional prepositioning, regular deployments of U.S. strike aircraft, and command and control arrangements. Despite Qatar's warm welcome, putting all the eggs we now have in Saudi Arabia into the single Qatari basket is a risk that requires careful consideration, given lingering uncertainties about Qatar's long-term reliability.

Over the longer term, there are possibilities that could be pursued with Oman and possibly the United Arab Emirates (UAE). None of these locations, either singly or in combination, could ever replace Saudi Arabia entirely. Nonetheless, as discussed below, deemphasizing the military component of the U.S.-Saudi relationship could have a positive effect on political development in the Kingdom and therefore in addressing the underlying causes of terrorism in the Islamic world.

Another reason to maintain our present capabilities at least as long as Saddam Husayn is in power is that any effort to remove him that envisions the possible use of military force would be hampered without the bases, infrastructure, airspace, and geographic depth than can best be provided by Saudi Arabia in particular and its neighbors in general. Saddam could be ousted without access to Saudi Arabia, but it would be more difficult, costly, and time-consuming, particularly if the United States could not use facilities in Turkey to support military operations. Without Saudi Arabia, a land assault would necessarily be conducted along a narrow, predictable front along the Kuwait-Iraq border, throwing away the U.S. advantage in high-speed maneuver, unless American ground forces were allowed to attack from Turkey. Without access to Saudi airspace, airborne warning and control systems, tankers, and other intelligence, command and control (C^2), and support aircraft would be forced to operate in tightly constrained orbits over Kuwait and the Gulf proper, dramatically reducing the proportion of Iraqi territory over which surveillance could be maintained and extending the range from targets at which tactical aircraft would be refueled. Finally, without access to Saudi infrastructure, supplying the force would be entirely dependent on a very limited number of Kuwaiti (and possibly southern Iraqi) seaports and airfields—curtailing throughput capacity, placing combat service support functions uncomfortably near the front, taking ramp space away from combat aircraft, and at best putting a large proportion of our eggs in a single basket. All of this is in addition to the negative political effect on other Gulf countries that Saudi noninvolvement would be likely to have.

New Basing Concepts

The Persian Gulf is a good candidate for exploring the feasibility and cost effectiveness of mobile offshore basing, and the Department of Defense should use joint experimentation and transformation funds to do a proof of concept study using the Gulf as a test bed. In the near term, it would be particularly useful to create C^2 capabilities afloat to improve combat redundancy and eliminate the ability of any regional state to veto U.S. operations by blocking access to command facilities. This process could be started by returning a C^2 ship to the Gulf to embark at least a portion of the Joint Task Force Southwest Asia headquarters, which is currently located in Saudi Arabia at Prince Sultan Air Base.

In principle, the United States might be able to reduce its profile further by conducting deterrence and containment of Iraq from bases outside the Gulf itself. However, the long-term sustainability of operating from over the horizon, in terms of cost and wear and tear on people and equipment, would need to be taken into account as well as the political signal implicit in a pullback from the Gulf. Rotating forces in and out of locations outside the Gulf, such as the Red Sea littoral, Jordan, and South Asia, could be worthwhile, particularly if the U.S. presence was periodic rather than continuous at any location. Militarily, this concept will become increasingly practicable as force transformation creates capabilities to deliver decisive force from longer range. In the more distant future, a mobile offshore base might be large enough to accommodate aircraft that currently fly out of Saudi locations.

Enhanced Combat Capabilities

Reducing the number and visibility of forward deployed forces while maintaining necessary military capabilities will require qualitative improvements of forward deployed capabilities. This is particularly true, given the political realities in the region, if the Army is to carry out the mandate in the 2001 *Quadrennial Defense Review* (QDR) *Report* to explore options for enhancing ground force capabilities in the Gulf. There are several priorities for force enhancements. First, defense against missile attacks should be bolstered. Additional PAC–3 units and high-tech aircraft for rapid strikes against WMD targets should be stationed in the region; forces deployed in the Gulf should have first claim on next-generation ballistic missile defense systems; and the Gulf should be used as a test bed for early deployment of emergency missile defense capabilities and for maintaining a continuous presence of these assets in the region. Second, steps should be taken to lessen the vulnerability of local bases and infrastructure to enemy missile strikes and related antiaccess/area denial threats. In addition to improved missile defenses, ports, airfields, and command posts should be hardened and diversified. Finally, efforts to create the spearhead force for the Gulf should be accelerated.

Deployment Patterns

The continuous presence of U.S. land-based forces at about five or six major fixed locations has undesirable political and operational consequences. It aggravates tensions with local populations, to whom U.S. force presence increasingly appears permanent rather than, as we advertise it, temporary. It creates a baseline against which any adversary can easily develop warning indicators—deployment of U.S. forces to any location outside the established pattern can safely be taken as a sign of impending action. Finally, while concentrating the presence at a few fortified locations simplifies the problem of providing ground combat units to defend them, it also presents would-be terrorists with lucrative, well-known targets. Consequently, the United States should reduce the visibility and predictability of such fixed deployments by moving to a rotational peacetime posture that relies on regular movements of Army, Air Force, and Navy units in and out of a wider variety of locations for operations and training and exercises with local forces. Deployments would be scheduled, under the QDR principle of global force presence policy, so that a particular capability is based at different locations over time.

Additionally, critical infrastructure would be replicated at multiple locations, enabling forces to be positioned in a number of possible configurations depending on the contingency and political circumstances. At the same time, U.S. forces need to find ways to minimize the scale of the infrastructure required, to accept that there are valid strategic reasons for keeping operations on an expeditionary basis, and to resist the perennial temptation to recreate in the Persian Gulf the kind of home-away-from-home environment that has characterized the American presence in Europe and the Far East since World War II. The United States should coordinate periodic deployments of allied forces to the Gulf with its own to bolster their overall deterrent value. The Air Force should regularly deploy strategic bombers to the region for joint and combined exercises; afloat, the Navy and Marine Corps should augment their presence by routinely dispatching reconfigured amphibious ready groups that combine amphibious assault ships with Aegis and cruise missile ships to create improved expeditionary strike forces.

Prepositioning

Prepositioning of heavy and bulky equipment remains the key to rapid reinforcement of the Gulf region and therefore to the eventual reduction in the number of regularly deployed forces. While substantial progress has been made in this area over the past decade, there is room for improving the flow rates for arriving U.S. forces to ensure rapid and decisive defeat of an adversary. Additional bare-base sets as well as additional Army brigade sets of equipment should be located at various airfields in the region; the other services should be directed to invest more heavily in equipment that would be prepositioned afloat in the region. Because of both political and operational factors, an expanded prepositioning program would be most successful if Saudi Arabia granted approval to place critical war reserve stocks in the Kingdom. Although the Saudis have rejected these proposals in the past, with some U.S. prodding they could come to see the political and military advantages of trading forces-in-place for prepositioned material.

To improve the climate for Saudi approval, the administration should seek legislative relief from constraints on U.S. flexibility to implement prepositioning programs in ways that would minimize the American footprint. For example, existing legislation is interpreted as requiring prepositioned material to be held under exclusive U.S. title, custody, and control. The Saudi Arabian government has consistently considered these conditions and the agreements that would be required to implement them an unacceptable infringement of Saudi sovereignty. Moreover, the legal barriers to allowing a host country to buy or lease equipment with the intention of storing it for the use of U.S. forces in an emergency are so cumbersome as to have defeated numerous attempts at innovation over the years, not only in Saudi Arabia but also throughout the Gulf.[1]

The United States should also reexamine its policy of excessive dependence on host-nation support for such prepositioning and infrastructure initiatives. While a reasonable degree of burdensharing is appropriate, the effect of American demands that Saudi Arabia and Kuwait (in particular) foot almost the entire bill for the U.S. presence has been to distort the U.S. Government's own budgetary and strategic decisionmaking processes—where assets are positioned often depends as much on whether the host will pick up the tab as on the strategic merits of the case. The tendency of the military departments to take maximum advantage of host-nation support as a means of conserving their own resources leads to frequent abuses of Saudi and Kuwaiti hospitality, while the Gulf states for their part often succumb to the temptation to view U.S. forces as hired help. Meanwhile, the fact that the host governments are spending large sums to support the presence of unpopular foreign forces is grist for the radical Islamists' propaganda mills. Finally, the friction is only aggravated by the lack of a common strategic perspective within which both sides could appreciate the contributions of the other to the common endeavor.

Regional Security Cooperation

The least successful of all the elements of the security strategy on which the United States embarked after the Gulf War has been developing Gulf state capabilities to provide for their own defense, individually and collectively. In this area, they have failed to live up to even the modest expectations set forth in U.S. planning. As highlighted in chapter four, overcoming obstacles to improving regional security cooperation will be difficult. It is unrealistic to expect the Gulf states to defend the region against major aggression without U.S. military intervention. But this is the wrong standard to apply: it is not unreasonable for GCC states to provide forces to delay a major attack and inflict costs on an aggressor and to be capable of handling minor regional contingencies (for example, raids on off-shore oil installations) without relying on American forces. A number of steps could be taken to redress shortfalls in GCC capabilities. For instance, the United States could:

- discourage the Gulf states from focusing their attention on unrealistic and ineffective standing multilateral forces such as Peninsula Shield at the expense of developing force specialization and niche capabilities.
- authorize the provision of military assistance directly to the GCC as "an international organization, the assisting of which the President finds will strengthen the security of the United States and promote world peace."[2] Providing training and supplies (such as communications equipment, publications, and C^2 systems) to the GCC as a whole, rather than individually to its members, would enable the United States to help build the organization's institutional capabilities and credibility.
- adjust the U.S. Central Command exercise program to encourage intra-GCC cooperation; instead of trying to develop U.S. exercises with the GCC as a group, priority should be given to developing trilateral and quadrilateral exercises with forces from the United States.
- encourage the GCC to adopt selected North Atlantic Treaty Organization standardization agreements to promote interoperability. The GCC states lack the capability to replicate the alliance standardization process, but this is not a standard to which they need be held.
- explore ways of developing a combined GCC professional military education system to raise the standard of command and staff work, promote common doctrine, and build personal links among officers.
- develop legal authorities and procedures to allow limited noncrisis use of U.S.-owned assets by Gulf forces when doing so would enhance regional stability and security. For example, U.S. Naval Forces Central Command has proposed in the past that the UAE and

Oman navies be allowed to crew and operate U.S. Navy mine warfare vessels when they are not required for contingency operations. Mechanisms should be developed to permit this and similar initiatives.[3]

Coalition Forces

The United States should also try to improve extraregional contributions to Gulf security. The GCC states are unlikely to accept a major role for non-Gulf Arab regimes in regime security, which would put their security at the mercy of the vagaries of inter-Arab politics. Nevertheless, while there are formidable political and operational obstacles to developing Arab expeditionary capabilities, there would be a substantial payoff if Islamic countries (for example, Egypt, Pakistan, Jordan, and Morocco) increased their potential contribution to Gulf security. The United States could facilitate this outcome without resort to the formal arrangements that have proven ineffective in the past by, for example, restructuring the U.S.-Egyptian security assistance program to emphasize the capability to deploy a significant Egyptian force using U.S. (or allied) lift in a regional crisis; and exercising Egyptian, Jordanian, and other capabilities to deploy small heavy forces to hot spots, including refocusing the biennial *Bright Star* exercise with Egypt.

Beyond Saddam

Looking beyond a change of the Iraqi regime, the military and political calculus about the continuing U.S. presence that might be required in the longer run will depend on how that change takes place—with or without a U.S. military occupation of Iraq—and what kind of government succeeds Saddam Husayn. Four alternatives suggest themselves:

The *European or East Asian model*, under which the United States is viewed as the only credible and acceptable stabilizing force for a critical region. This assumes that either Iraq or Iran, if not both, would continue to present a threat to U.S. interests even under less objectionable regimes and that the GCC states, as suggested in chapter four, would be unwilling or unable to develop their own capabilities to meet those threats. Under this alternative, the United States would seek long-term access to shore bases for a robust but reduced ground and air presence—probably about a composite air wing and a heavy battalion task force—that would continue into the foreseeable future. In addition, this alternative would envision the presence in the Gulf of a carrier task force most if not all the time.

An *over-the-horizon presence*, similar to the normal arrangement pre-1990 but with greater diversification of bed-down locations. The

United States would attempt, through diplomacy and other means, to ensure that Iraq and Iran balance each other in such a way that neither is strong enough to challenge U.S. vital interests. Meanwhile, the United States would attempt to strengthen friendly forces and ensure through prepositioning and exercises that American and coalition forces could return rapidly in a crisis.

A *combination of reliance on local and U.S. capabilities*, based on the assumption that the regional situation would not tolerate a continuing U.S. military presence at anything resembling the levels of the past. Enhancements to local forces would be combined with active encouragement of better regional cooperation, continued improvements in American ability to deploy rapidly, and a continuing force presence well below the normal levels of the past 12 years, maintained through a series of deployments shifting among various locations.

A complete *strategic shift*, based on changes in either U.S.-Iraqi or U.S.-Iranian relations. The United States would align with a friendly regime in either Baghdad or Tehran, relying on that alignment to keep the peace. U.S. relations with its present Arab security partners would become primarily economic, depending on a shared interest in the sale of their oil on world markets to maintain the flow of energy resources.

All of these options continue to posit the United States as an external balancer, offsetting possible threats to stability; they differ only in the level of effort necessary to achieve that condition.

Terrorism and Domestic Change

Another critical variable in determining American success in bringing peace and stability to the Persian Gulf and in uprooting terrorism there is how effectively regional governments respond to pressures for domestic change. Regardless of whether the Saddam Husayn regime remains in place or of the strategic character and intentions of the government that might succeed his regime, fighting terrorism needs to become a central element in the redefinition of U.S. security strategy in the Gulf.

There are obvious connections between U.S. strategy toward Iraq, the global war on terrorism, U.S. military presence in the Gulf, and the Middle East peace process. Neither the Israeli-Palestinian conflict nor the U.S. military presence is the fundamental cause of Islamic-based anti-Western terrorism, but they are catalysts for it. At a minimum, the prominent place given to U.S. military presence in the catalogue of grievances used by terrorist organizations and their sympathizers to mobilize support for their agenda suggests that the United States has to weigh the direct military advantage of having troops on the ground in the Gulf for an extended period of time against the potential political costs in terms of attitudes toward the United States, the survivability of the regimes on which we currently depend for access, and the need for greater political pluralism and toleration. A large U.S. military presence is an impediment to such orderly political evolution for four reasons:

- The larger and more visible the presence, the more likely it is that accidents, misconduct, or just the inconvenience and noise associated with military operations will provide a rallying point around radical elements.
- The presence of U.S. troops tends to associate the ruling families with a host of deeply unpopular U.S. policies—sanctions and possibly war against Iraq, support of Israel against the Palestinians, and the perceived American campaign against Islam, to name the three most obvious. This generally has the effect of weakening the legitimacy of the existing governments, lending credibility to their and our most radical opponents, and discouraging regimes from loosening control over public discourse.
- While a policy of constructive ambiguity has allowed the United States and its hosts to cooperate while maintaining substantially different interpretations of the justification for the U.S. military presence, it also leads both sides to believe they are doing the other a favor. Each therefore believes it holds a political "account receivable" against the other. Host governments tend to assume this debt is payable in the form of a U.S. guarantee of rulers' survival on their thrones. The ruling families might take pressures for change more seriously if they were less sure that they had an American insurance policy in their pockets.
- Finally, U.S. dependence on host governments for access to defend U.S. interests impedes Washington's ability to talk straight on matters of human rights and political reform. At a minimum, it creates the widespread impression that the United States is sacrificing principle to expediency and, in the eyes of some in the region, makes the United States complicit in whatever repression is practiced.

Conclusion

For the United States, there is no escaping the role of security guarantor of the Gulf for the foreseeable future. But trying to guarantee that security through a large-scale, visible, and seemingly permanent U.S. presence will erode security, undermine security relationships with key Gulf states, impede needed political reforms, stir domestic opposition within Saudi Arabia and other Gulf states, and feed anti-American Islamic extremism. With or without regime change in Iraq, the U.S. military posture toward the Persian Gulf will require significant adjustments over the next decade. The future of Iraq will be the key driver of the size and character of these changes.

Regardless of how regime change occurs in Iraq—whether it happens quickly and decisively or is protracted and messy—the United States will need to diversify its dependence for regional basing and access and reduce the visibility and predictability of its force presence. In the long term, the drastic reduction or elimination of the Iraqi threat to the region is the sine qua non for success in guaranteeing the security of the Gulf while reducing the political costs that the U.S. military presence imposes on other U.S. interests and our Gulf partners. While more aggressive efforts to unseat Saddam would not be cost-free, neither are the alternatives. Either a continuation of the policy of active containment or a policy of retrenched defense and deterrence would require the maintenance of a significant military presence in the Gulf, with all its attendant political and security risks for both the Gulf Arab countries and the United States. Moreover, the longer the United States needs military access to the Gulf states to deal with a continuing Iraqi threat, the longer it will be identified with some Gulf regimes' resistance to political evolution.

In the absence of successful regime change in Iraq, the transformation of military capabilities provides a way to guarantee security while reducing the U.S. military footprint, but the adjustment of our profile will need to be carried out before the promise of transformation can be realized. Unfortunately, time is not on the American side: if left to his own devices, Saddam will become more threatening in the years ahead. Thus, until Saddam disappears from the scene and Iraq is no longer a menace to U.S. interests and regional security, there is scope for reengineering the U.S. force posture, but it would be foolhardy to make significant reductions in U.S. forward deployed forces.

If the continued survival of the Saddam Husayn regime extracts huge costs for regional security, success in removing him and his circle would yield an enormous payoff. It would not eliminate all problems from the region, but it would drastically reduce the requirement for U.S. military forces to deal with the problems that remained. It would give

Iraq the opportunity to develop, for the first time in decades, a system of government that would not depend on a permanent state of hostility with its neighbors to justify its domestic power structure. It would allow the United States and the Gulf Arabs to return their relationships to a more normal footing, free of many of the irritants that inevitably arise from the presence of foreign forces in an alien culture. Most importantly, it would provide the opportunity for the Gulf states, and others in the Middle East, to develop and nurture new institutions and processes, firmly rooted in the religious and cultural legacy of the region, that will allow their people to thrive and prosper in the 21st century. Only by doing so can they hope to escape the cycle of warfare, repression, and terrorism that was the lot of so many of them throughout the previous century. In other words, maintaining the current status quo in the Gulf has its own costs and is not sustainable over the next decade. The costs of not going to war to oust Saddam Husayn need to be more fully appreciated.

Of course, the potential benefits of toppling Saddam will need to be carefully weighed against the risks of a U.S. invasion and the substantial costs to the United States if it has to occupy Iraq for an indefinite period in order to ensure a stable transition, maintain order and Iraq's territorial integrity, protect the new regime, and demilitarize Iraq's armed forces to eliminate their offensive potential. With or without regime change in Iraq, however, the United States needs to fashion a post-containment strategy that reduces the political, diplomatic, and military burdens, on both the United States and our Gulf state partners, of meeting America's security responsibilities. However, reducing U.S. reliance on Saudi Arabia as an operating location should not be confused with intentionally rupturing the U.S.-Saudi political-military partnership.

While the United States would do well to diversify the countries upon which it depends and to create redundant capabilities in multiple locations, it should do so out of military and political prudence, not as a step toward jettisoning the Saudi relationship. Saudi Arabia needs to remain an important pillar of U.S. security strategy for the region, but one that the United States puts less weight on in the future, for several reasons. Its political stature in the Islamic world, the fact that its regime is the ultimate target for many of the terrorists, and, perhaps most importantly, the fact that the ideological, financial, and personal roots of al Qaeda *are* within Saudi Arabia give the Kingdom an inescapable role in both the global war on terrorism and in generating Arab-Islamic support for other U.S. priorities from Iraq to the peace process. Above all, the eastern province of Saudi Arabia is the center of gravity of global petroleum trade, the security of which is the reason we are in the Gulf in the first place. Put simply, the U.S.-Saudi relationship needs to be repaired rather than trashed.

The best course of action for protecting American interests in the Persian Gulf is to encourage evolutionary adaptation. Squaring a tangible and immediate national interest in stability with a less tangible interest in democracy is difficult everywhere, but it is an especially delicate task in the Gulf. It must be done, nevertheless, because initiating orderly change toward greater political participation and reconciling deeply traditional social structures with the realities of the modern global system, while not without risk, are the only ways to forestall serious instability in the long run.

Notes

[1] There is legal authority for the United States to earmark and preposition U.S.-owned materiel for other countries' use in wartime, known as War Reserve Stocks for Allies, but not for other countries to do the same for the United States.

[2] Under existing law, "The President is authorized to furnish military assistance, on such terms and conditions as he may determine, to any friendly country or international organization, the assisting of which the President finds will strengthen the security of the United States and promote world peace."

[3] Existing U.S. law allows giving military equipment to certain countries on a grant basis, but what the law authorizes as "loans" are in fact rentals. For either a loan or a lease, the receiving country must reimburse the U.S. Government for depreciation of the equipment plus any out-of-pocket expenses.

About the Contributors

Richard L. Kugler is distinguished research professor at the Center for Technology and National Security Policy at the National Defense University. He has held a number of senior positions in the Department of Defense and RAND. He is the author or editor of 15 books on U.S. national security and defense strategy and has published numerous articles in leading journals and newspapers. Recently, he co-edited *The Global Century: Globalization and National Security* (National Defense University Press, 2001).

Kenneth M. Pollack is director of research at the Saban Center for Middle East Policy at The Brookings Institution. He has served formerly as director for Persian Gulf Affairs at the National Security Council, Persian Gulf military analyst at the Central Intelligence Agency, and senior research professor at the National Defense University. He has published numerous articles on Middle East political-military affairs and is author of *Arabs at War: Military Effectiveness, 1948–1991* (University of Nebraska Press, 2002) and *The Threatening Storm: The Case for Invading Iraq* (Random House, 2002).

Joseph McMillan is a distinguished research fellow in the Institute for National Strategic Studies at the National Defense University. He formerly served in the Office of the Under Secretary of Defense for Policy as country director for Near East and South Asian Affairs, country director for the former Soviet Union, principal director of the Office of Russian, Ukrainian, and Eurasian affairs, and principal director of the Office of Near East and South Asian Affairs. He is the author of *U.S.-Saudi Relations: Rebuilding the Strategic Consensus* (National Defense University Press, 2001).

Eugene B. Rumer is a senior research fellow in the Institute for National Strategic Studies at the National Defense University. Previously, he was a visiting fellow at the Washington Institute for Near East Policy, a member of the Policy Planning staff at the Department of State, director of Russian, Ukrainian, and Eurasian Affairs at the National Security Council, and a senior analyst at RAND. He has published numerous articles on Russia and U.S.-Russian relations and is the author of *Dangerous Drift: Russia's Middle East Policy* (Washington Institute for Near East Policy, 2000).

Richard D. Sokolsky is a distinguished research fellow in the Institute for National Strategic Studies at the National Defense University. He served formerly as a senior fellow at RAND, director of the Office of Defense Relations and Security Assistance in the Department of State, and Persian Gulf analyst on the State Department Policy Planning staff. He has published numerous articles on American foreign policy and is the co-author of *Persian Gulf Security: Improving Allied Military Contributions* (RAND, 2001) and *NATO and Caspian Security: A Mission Too Far?* (RAND, 1999).

Judith S. Yaphe is a senior research fellow in the Institute for National Strategic Studies (INSS) at the National Defense University. Before joining INSS in 1995, Dr. Yaphe was a senior political analyst for the U.S. Government and received the Intelligence Medal of Commendation for her work on Iraq and the Gulf War. She has published numerous articles on Iraq, Iran, and the Persian Gulf and is co-author of *Strategic Implications of a Nuclear-Armed Iran* (National Defense University Press, 2001) and editor of *The Middle East in 2015: The Impact of Regional Trends on U.S. Strategic Planning* (National Defense University Press, 2002).